WORDS WANTED

WORDS WANTED

By

EUNICE V. PIKE

MOODY PRESS

CHICAGO

Contents

CHAPTER I

From Beyond the Mountains

(SPRING OF 1940)

"POOR EUNICE, white skin is not any good," Marta murmured as she pulled gently on the skin of my sunburned, peeling arm. She chuckled as a piece came off in her fingers. Her face alight with interest, she touched the white flesh that had been shaded by my sleeve, then she touched the tanned portion. Firmly now, she rubbed her finger across the dividing line.

"It is very ugly," she said gently.

That little episode had interrupted one of my language lessons Marta was supposed to be teaching me, but the hunt for words frequently was postponed while we learned each other's customs. She learned about Americans, and I about the beliefs and life of the Mazatecs.

My purpose for studying both the language and the customs of the Mazatec Indians was to translate the New Testament for them. The tribe is one of about fifty in Mexico that are still speaking the language they used before the arrival of the Spanish conqueror, Hernando Cortez. In spite of the fact that Spanish is spoken throughout Mexico, remnants of those tribes still cling to their own original languages. In 1940 the Mazatecs numbered about 65,000 and 90 percent of them spoke no Spanish.

My partner, Florrie Hansen, and I were members of the Wycliffe Bible Translators, and when we first arrived in Mexico almost nothing was known about the Mazatec language. Three and a half years later we were talking it—with lots of errors—had figured out something of the grammar, and had our opinions about the alphabet with which it should be written. With that temporary alphabet we had started a Mazatec dictionary by making a file with a 3 by 5 slip of paper for each new word. Day by day we watched it grow as our knowledge of the language increased.

Sometimes while working on that dictionary-file my fingers were clumsy with cold, for the town of Chalco was 6,000 feet above sea level and the thermometer—both inside and out—frequently registered in the fifties. When it was foggy or rainy I wore so many clothes that I had to reroute my spoon in its trip from the plate to my mouth.

On one of those cold days Inés, another Indian neighbor, came in. Seeing my wraps she commented on how nice and warm I must be. She herself was dressed in an ankle-length blue and white cotton skirt. Over the top she had a muslin tunic that had been embroidered with flowers and birds. It was made even more colorful with several rows of pink and blue ribbon. It was the traditional costume for Chalco, and it was beautiful, but a person had to be born to it, if she were to survive that climate in such an outfit.

Because of my wraps Inés expected my hands to

be warm, and she reached for them. She found them to be like ice in comparison with hers. Taking them between her own, she blew on them gently, and as she blew I felt the chill leaving. In between breaths she said, "You are like a stone."

I objected, "But a stone is warm sometimes."

"That is why I said it. A stone is warm when the sun shines, and cold when it does not."

She had a point. That day she found my hands cold, but she remembered that I had sunburned as I had ridden horseback in from Tepetlán, the town that connected Chalco with the rest of the world.

In that town so far from automobiles, window glass, and other symbols of modern civilization, many people had never seen an egg beater, a typewriter, or a stove. It was not that Chalco itself was so small—it had a population of about 2,000—but it took a ten-hour horseback ride to get over the mountains. The people were curious about anything that came in from beyond those mountains, and Florrie and I fitted into that category. They were fascinated by our things, and they liked to watch us.

Those with the best opportunity were Esteban and Catarina, our landlords. They lived just to the right of us with their twelve-year-old adopted son Marcos, and their seven-year-old nephew Tomás. Tomás' father and mother had died, and they were bringing him up as their own.

On our left Marta was in charge of the household. She had been in her teens when her home collapsed in a windstorm. It had killed her parents, so it was Marta who had brought up the family. Things were easier now since her younger sister had married, and her brother Ramón had become man size.

Other families lived above and below us on the mountainside and they were part of our audience the day we unpacked our victrola. In the beginning I was careful of it, always starting and stopping it myself, but their enthusiasm wore me out. By the time the morning was over, I was glad to have anyone do it.

Along toward the middle of the afternoon, after all the records had been played several times, Tomás asked, "Is that man's voice tired?"

"No."

"Then let us play them all over again." Tomás asked the questions for the whole crowd, but they listened to the answers as carefully as he did.

His next question was, "Is a man inside?"

"No. The man sang in front of a machine that put a mark on a disk like this. Now when this disk is put on another machine it makes his voice speak again."

"Oh!" Silence for a while, then, "Suppose the man died, then what?"

"His voice would still talk from the record."

"Oh," said he with awe.

Our radio also impressed the neighbors. As they listened that first evening, we pointed out some of the noises to Tomás and Marcos. At one station someone was singing, then the announcer spoke, a twist of the dial and some tap dancers came in. I told the boys that people were dancing and that the noise we heard was their feet rapping on the floor.

"People dancing? Where?" Tomás walked around the table and peered at the radio from all angles.

Marcos had been silent most of the time while he listened to an announcer, a soloist, and a quartet. Now he spoke up. "What I cannot understand is how so many get inside all at once." Our explanation that the people were singing and talking in a city far away did not satisfy.

The radio we had bought for our own enjoyment —we wanted to hear the news. The victrola was for the people—we wanted them to hear the records put out by Gospel Recordings, Inc. We did not have any records in Mazatec yet, but even the Bible stories in Spanish served as a purpose, for Florrie or I gave a brief summary in Mazatec as they played. One of the people's favorites was "The Ninety and Nine." They heard the shepherd count, heard him call, and then the soft bleating of the little lost sheep. They enjoyed the sound effects as they came from the victrola, and through our translation they learned that the Lord loved them.

Little Tomás found so many exciting things in our house that he was in and out all day long. If we were getting dinner, he might be content just to sit and watch us work, and if we were at our desks studying, he might look at a picture book, or put a puzzle together. I could concentrate pretty well when he was playing by himself, but not after he had tired of his play and stood leaning against my desk. When his mood changed to a playful teasing one, he deliberately bothered even though he knew I wanted to study. One day as he passed my chair,

I reached out and caught him and held him against the back of it.

"There now!" I told him. "I have got you and I am not going to let you go!" He tried to pull away, but he could not break my hold.

"Let me go!" he said. Then he saw a fly on the wall, and he stopped struggling. This time he said, "See that fly? Kill that fly! He'll pay for me." He was bringing into his play the lessons he had learned about Christ. Although the idea to us was fantastic, he was comparing Christ with the fly. Christ had no sin—the fly had not bothered me. Christ died to pay for our sins—I was to kill the fly. And we, because of Christ's death, are freed. Tomás waited quietly for me to release him. And I did.

He ran outside, and Florrie and I looked at each other, thrilled with his understanding. Then Florrie snapped to attention. "That's the word for redeem!" But we had forgotten what he had said. We called him in again. "Tomás, what did you say just now?"

"I said, 'Let me go.' "

"Oh, no, Tomás." Florrie and I both spoke in quick distress. Could it be that even after having heard it we would still miss out on that important word *redeem*? I tried to jog his memory, "You said, 'See that fly? . . .' "

This time he repeated the sentence we wanted. We wrote it down immediately and he went out with a half-disgusted, "Always wanting words." He was right. Whether we were buying food in the market, chatting with one of our friends, or entertaining the neighbor children, we were listening for words—those words that were still needed for the New Testament.

Florrie turned to the Table of Contents at the front of her Bible and studied the figures she had written there. Months before she had added up the number of verses contained in each of the different books and she had recorded the totals for future reference. Sometimes she referred back to them with a sigh. "How long will it take to translate the New Testament into the Mazatec language?" That day she tried to be more specific. "Once Mark, Luke, John, and Acts are done, the whole New Testament is half done," she observed hopefully. Then she became still more specific. "There are 7,957 verses in all; Mark, Luke, John, and Acts make up a total of 3,715—half is 3,978." Then almost unwillingly she admitted, "Of course that is just taking the actual number of verses into consideration. The Epistles are much harder to translate than the Gospels."

In spite of that, Florrie was estimating that we might complete a first draft of the New Testament within the next year. It would be very imperfect, perhaps not even worthy of the name *milestone,* but if we had been all the way through it once, we would at least become aware of the words that were still lacking. If we had a mental list of the English words, perhaps we would notice their Mazatec equivalents when someone used them in our presence.

As we worked together, Florrie and I observed that she spent more time at translation than I did, while I, perhaps because of my nursing background, spent more time with the people. Satisfied that both were necessary, we agreed that she would see the translation done, while I would teach the people to use it.

The difference was one of emphasis rather than one of activity, for she still taught people, and I kept my interest in translation. But because of that emphasis, she was doing the first draft of all but Revelation and Colossians. I chose to do Colossians in order to get a taste of a really hard book—but I was glad it was short. I chose Revelation because I had been told that it was easiest—in it the Apostle John described what he saw, and although the implications were difficult to understand, the words were not.

The phrase *to judge* was one that baffled both of us every time it occurred. We had asked the Mazatecs about their local court, about the more powerful county court, about the gossiping neighbors, about the village peacemaker, but none of the words obtained through those discussions had satisfied us. We had also asked some of the Mazatecs who had been to school for a translation of the word from Spanish, but in spite of their education, a very scant one, we could not be sure that they knew the meaning of the Spanish word they were trying to translate.

We tried again with a different type of illustration. "Listen, Catarina," we said to our landlady, who was also one of our language informants, "God is up in Heaven, and He looks down on earth and sees a man, and He says, 'That is a good man.' Then He sees another man and He says, 'That man

is a liar.' Then He sees another man and He says,
'I will not give that man a prize, he is lazy and does
not do My work.' " Catarina looked startled as our
illustration progressed, but when we asked, "What
is God doing?" she answered without hesitation,
"We say that God is making accounts." That
sounded right for that illustration, but it did not
have the broad general idea of the English *to judge*.
It was just another word to add to the list of related
words that we had already obtained: "he criticizes,"
"he punishes," "he accuses," "he arbitrates." We
kept on trying and in some places in the New Testament we used one word, and in some places we
used another. All the time we were hoping that
eventually we would find one Mazatec word that
would include all those ideas.

One of our best language helpers was the girl who
had warmed my hands, Inés. She knew no Spanish
and had never been to school, but two years before,
we had started to teach her to read. She loved it
and came every day for a lesson in spite of funerals
or weddings—the social engagements that turned
aside so many other Mazatecs. Her persistence had
been rewarded, and this girl who had been illiterate
two years before now read with comparative fluency. Of her whole tribe, she was the first and until
then the only monolingual to read in her own language.

As her reading ability had increased, she had become more and more valuable to us, for we used her
as a means of checking a Mazatec's reaction to a
written page. Florrie had typed up a copy of the
newly translated Gospel of John, and as Inés read

it, Florrie sat at her elbow, alert to the expression on her face as well as to any comments she might make. Was the meaning intelligible to her, or was it hidden in disconnected or incorrect words? When in doubt, Florrie questioned her and marked the places needing revision.

While reading, Inés leaned over the page, and as long as she understood, almost nothing distracted her. At other times a puzzled look grew on her face until at last she relaxed and announced, "I do not understand."

That was Florrie's cue to explain in other words the meaning of the verse. As Inés became satisfied, Florrie almost invariably questioned, "How should I have said it?" When Inés could tell her, the correction was written in. When she could not, the place was marked for further study with one of our other informants.

At times Inés' comment on Florrie's explanation was, "So that's what that word means." Such a statement always left Florrie dissatisfied, and the dialogue which followed went something like this:

"Is it not a good word?"

"Why, yes, probably so."

"Then why didn't you understand it?"

Inés' disgust was apparent. "Do you understand all the words of your language?"

"No."

"Then why should I understand all of mine?" And she would tell us what we had been told many times before, that "only a few old men" knew all the words. For that reason Inés thought the word should stand, but we were tempted to change it.

We did not want a translation that could be used only by the intellectual giants of the tribe. A New Testament understandable by all was our goal. We hoped that through it the Mazatecs would come to know Christ, and that they would try to please Him in their everyday lives.

CHAPTER II

Fire

(SPRING OF 1940)

SOMETIMES WHEN I LOOKED at the language data we had worked so hard to gather, I silently prayed that the Lord would protect it. Since much of it was the original handwritten data, it was evident that a little fire could destroy years of work. Whenever we typed anything, we made carbon copies and tried to keep those copies in different places, but our dictionaries were made up from words and phrases which had been added day by day and they remained handwritten.

Usually we typed any materials that we wanted the Mazatecs to read, for they had not learned to read our handwriting. We had made copies of the primer, some Bible stories, a few selected verses, the whole Gospel of John; but we still had only the original of the other books of the New Testament. We had written the verses on separate 3 by 5 slips of paper, and had filed them according to books. The file was helpful because in it we could locate easily any verse needed, and could also add alternate translations without disturbing the first one. The slips were kept in a metal cabinet, but even that did not seem safe to me and, since our house had a thatched roof, it probably was not.

I looked at the thatched roof over our heads. Layer after layer of sugarcane leaves had been doubled over a bamboo framework until it was a bushy twelve inches thick. It was beautiful, but I had been told that if it caught fire it would burn hot and fast.

The walls of our hut were of adobe and we knew they would not burn. They were chipped by the thirty years' use they had had before our arrival, but they were still sturdy. The roof rested on beams which extended a few inches beyond the walls. Wind made use of the open space between them and the roof, and came in boldly to flicker our candle, or to rustle the papers on our desks.

In our one-room hut (13 by 22 feet) we could not afford to let space go to waste, and we discovered that a box would just fit under the thatch and on top of the thick adobe wall. That helped relieve the congested floor space below, but it still left us in doubt as to what we should do with our kerosene and gasoline. In spite of fire hazards we felt we needed the kerosene for cooking and the gasoline for our study lamp. We finally set the fuel close enough to the door so that it would get lots of air, but far enough inside so that our guests would not drop cigarette ashes on it. We figured that in case of fire we would go out the window; since it had no glass to hinder, it would just be a matter of jumping through.

It was nice that we didn't have to see our own house burn to learn what such a fire would be like. One night after we were in bed Catarina called at the door, "Come, see! House burning!" We threw on some clothes and hurried outside. Down the hill from us a great column of sparks and smoke was rising straight into the air. The burning house was hidden from view by intervening ones, but even so we could see the flames following the sparks into the air. It was right in the center of town, and we knew that the other houses were in danger. Even as we watched, figures appeared on the roofs of the surrounding huts. Silhouetted against the brightened sky, we could see them seated, one on each ridge pole. They were waiting, ready to pounce on any sparks that might fall on the thatch.

A crowd was collecting as men became volunteer fire fighters. We could hear them shouting instructions to one another, and because their words came with gasps and jerks, we knew that they were working hard and fast. They were not attempting to put out the roof fire, rather they were trying to save the rest of the house by tearing it down. The walls were made of pine boards but, like many Mazatec huts, it had not been put up with hammer and nails. The framework had been tied together with vines and strips of bark, and the door had ropes for hinges. The men slashed the vines with their machetes and killed the flames by beating the freed piece against the ground. This whack, whack of the boards was the most outstanding sound of the moment.

The sparks from the burning house were beginning to lessen, when we heard the cry of, "Other house! Other house!" A second house had caught and sparks and smoke rose into the sky in another great column. With the men already there, this house was torn down before the walls had caught. There was a crash and an increase in the flying sparks as the corner posts were removed and the roof fell. Then the fire died quickly.

The men had not used water, for there was little or none to be had. Even drinking water had to be carried from a spring five minutes away. With a handicap like that, all of us were thankful that there had been no wind that night.

The following week we did have a big wind. Big enough to crumple some of the tin roofs on the merchants' stores and to carry away some of the thatch on others. Leaves of a sugarcane thatch are long and narrow, and usually nothing is needed to hold them in place, but that wind ruffled a number of roofs.

The leaves of our own house had been disarranged, and when I looked at it from the outside, it reminded me of a child whose hair needed combing. On the inside, we could stand by the stove and look through spaces to the sky. We showed Esteban, our landlord, and he brought in a long pole and poked and moved the leaves gently this way and that. With very little effort the leaves were adjusted and the holes covered again.

It was handy to have a landlord whose house was about six feet from ours when the roof needed to be readjusted, but there were times when I wished there was more distance between us and our close neighbors. I had thoughts like that almost every time I went out to burn trash. For the neighbor children this was great sport, and as soon as one of them saw me outside with the wastepaper basket he would give a shout for the others, "She's going to burn paper!"

It didn't matter what the children happened to be doing at the moment, they would stop a game of marbles, or stop mimicking a funeral parade in order to stand by the fire. Frequently one of them would say solemnly, "Your house will catch fire." But that solemn warning was the extent of their caution. If one of them chanced to see a "pretty paper" in the fire, he snatched at it eagerly. One child pulling at burning paper is bad enough, but when two or three get in a fight over the prize, it endangers the whole town. I learned to carry a little stick which served several purposes. I could hold down papers during a gust of wind, I could stir the fire as it was dying down, or I could ward off little hands unable to resist an imagined treasure.

I also learned what the neighbor children considered treasures: a bit of string, the box the toothpaste came in, any piece of paper with a picture on it, any piece of paper that would blow in the breeze —"a kite." I learned what the grownups wanted, for they sometimes stood around the fire too. They wanted any cardboard carton; if it was clean, they would keep their clothes in it; if it was old and soiled, they would park a hen under it at night. Mothers with little children wanted any kind of paper, either wrinkled torn pieces, or whole newspapers; they would put a few under their babies at night and it helped keep the bedding clean.

Once I had learned what they wanted I tried to give things away before they ever reached the wastebasket, but some things I did not want scattered over the neighborhood, and I insisted that they burn. So the children stood by, and when the fire had died down, they would jump in the middle of the ash heap, dancing with their bare feet in a race to see who could stamp out the most sparks.

Well, burning trash was not so different from anything else we did among the Mazatecs. It was all tied in with learning the Indian language. When the children called, "She is going to burn paper," they used one word for *burn*. When they said, "Your house will burn," it was another. As they warned each other, "You will burn your feet," that was still another.

So at least once a week I had practice switching— and hearing them switch—from *burn* which was a transitive verb, to *burn* which was intransitive, to *burn* which they used when speaking of flesh. It was sort of handy that lessons did not stop just because we had left the desk.

CHAPTER III

The Neighbors

(SPRING OF 1940)

As OUR KNOWLEDGE of the language increased, we learned that the Mazatecs actually had two sets of customs and beliefs. There were the deep-seated ones of their tribe, and those that had been superimposed by the Spanish-speaking people. To an outsider the latter were the more apparent, but it took a knowledge of both to really understand the meaning behind many of their words.

"Coyote!" said Catarina, her whole body alert. "Coyote," the others in the room agreed. To me it had sounded like a dog barking, but when I said so their "no" was sharp and final. Their apprehension was not just because a coyote sometimes stole chickens, but because (according to them) the god who lived at the top of the nearby mountain kept coyotes the same way a man keeps dogs. When the coyotes barked that was a sign that the mountain god was close by. He was supposed to be a kind god, but people noticed that sometimes a person died a day or two after a coyote had been there.

Certain people of town claimed that they could contact the mountain god, and they went through procedure for some of the people who wanted to get rich. They would sacrifice a chicken as a gift for him, or bribe him with other things.

Supposedly all the hilltops had gods, and every little spring and brook had demons. The water spirits were reportedly the more harmful and so the people paid them the most attention. They would bury turkey eggs in the ground, trying to persuade the water spirits to give back a sick relative's soul. Sometimes they would bury cocoa beans (money in the spirit world) trying to bribe the demons to kill some specified enemy. But even though they paid them well, they could not trust those water spirits. If an enemy paid more than they did, the evil might come back upon their own heads.

I never heard anything bad about their sun-god. They usually spoke of him with gratitude. They might say, "If it was not for him, we would walk as blind men." Or, "His radiance warms us." In fact, when we spoke of our Lord, they were apt to attribute everything we said to their sun-god. That confusion had started centuries ago when their ancestors first heard of Jesus. They accepted news of Him as befitting their sun-god and equated the two as one. That is, to them Jesus was the sun.

Marta was beginning to understand that there was a difference. She had been helping me to translate some Bible stories, reading aloud from the Spanish New Testament as she did it. She understood only a few of the Spanish words, and when she reached "gave thanks" in Matthew 15:36-39, she asked, "What does that mean?"

"You have seen us do that at mealtimes," I ex-

plained. "God gave us the food, so we thank Him
before we eat it."

"What do you say?" She was delighted for the
excuse to ask. She repeated the simple blessing after
me and said that from now on she would give
thanks too, but she lost interest and did not do it
very often.

Tomás prayed before eating. In fact, he would
slip up to our table and ask the Lord to bless our
food, even though he himself had eaten at home.
Such enthusiasm was typical of Tomás whether he
was memorizing Bible verses or making a top.

He would whittle for days on a piece of wood
trying to get it smooth and balanced. Then one
day I saw him make a top in a jiffy. He took an
empty wooden spool, cut it in half, and drove a peg
down through the hole. It was a top that hummed
at the twist of his fingers. But the name of the
gadget interested me almost as much as the fun he
was having with it. Its name was a compound word
made up of three parts, *top, wood,* and *thread.*
Each succeeding part modified the preceding part.
Thus it was a top made of wood that had something
to do with thread—a spool top.

Words like that showed me that it was important
to get the parts in their correct order. *Wood-thread*
meant a "spool," but *thread-wood* meant "sewing
thread" which needed to be distinguished from "em-
broidery thread" and "string."

Almost every day we learned something about
the language from the children who played in our
house. Marcos did not teach us as much as Tomás.
He was willing, but he was not the chatterbox that

Tomás was. Marcos was usually silent and he seldom smiled. Frequently his face was sullen and happiness far away. His was a hard life. Marcos was the youngest of a large family, his father having died when he was still small. His mother had been unable to carry the burden of so many children, and so she had given him to Esteban and Catarina. He was a hard-working boy, perhaps not so much from choice as necessity, for Esteban expected a man's work from him. Occasionally Esteban bragged about Marcos' strong arms. "He can hoe a field as fast as a man," he would say, but such compliments were rare. The more common remark was that Tomás was intelligent—his head was "soft," whereas Marcos' was "hard."

Catarina's preference for Tomás was apparent. It could be seen even in the boys' shirts. Tomás' were ironed, but Marcos' were left wrinkled. With Marcos, Esteban was a hard taskmaster, and when he was drunk, which was frequent, he sometimes enforced his words with blows. Perhaps as a reaction to his surroundings, Marcos became mean to his dog and to younger children.

Florrie and I could not see anything very lovely about Marcos' character, but when a person comes to believe on the Lord, he is completely reborn anyway. Once he believed, Marcos would have as good a starting point as anybody else. He was at a disadvantage when it came to learning about the Lord in that he was not reading very well. It would be a long time before he could ever read Scripture for himself. Perhaps he was too tired at the end of the day to concentrate. After awhile we almost stopped the formal reading lessons, but we continued a little each day, helping him with a Bible verse or two. We hoped that he would learn of the Lord's love even if his reading ability never improved.

It was during one of those lessons that a moth, attracted by our bright gasoline lamp and the light that streamed out between the wall and roof, came in to bombard our lamp. He slapped first one of us in the face and then the other as he zigzagged his crazy way. Now a moth does not hurt anybody. I have been slapped enough times so that I know. But back in those days I flinched whenever one wobbled past. Marcos saw my reaction, but instead of ridiculing me he reached out and grabbed it. Once he had it he was puzzled about what he should do next, so he held it out to me and said kindly, "Here is a bug." I wanted to shriek, "I do not want it!" but the expression on his face stopped me and I smiled instead, delighted that Marcos had chosen to be helpful.

CHAPTER IV

Because of Spanish

(SPRING OF 1940)

MOST OF THE PEOPLE of Chalco had a great desire to learn Spanish. Perhaps they thought they could acquire money faster if they knew some—it was true that many of the town's wealthiest citizens were either bilingual or had a smattering of Spanish. Perhaps the people wanted to be more one with the rest of Mexico—they knew that they would have to speak Spanish if they were to get along outside the Mazatec area. Whatever the reason, the more ambitious ones used every opportunity to learn a word or two.

That may have been the reason that Amalia, a twenty-year-old neighbor girl, became another reading pupil of ours. She arrived about five o'clock every afternoon, her Spanish New Testament tucked under her arm. She was interested in the Bible, but she hoped to learn a bit of Spanish too. We read a few verses of the Gospel of John together every afternoon. She read aloud, and then to check her understanding she told me in Mazatec what it had said. She needed some explanation with almost every verse, and even after I had helped her I wondered if she had really understood.

Then one afternoon we read from John 6. "Verily, verily, I say unto you, He that believeth on me hath everlasting life."

"Who has everlasting life?" I asked.

"Jesus."

"Yes. Who else? Do you?"

"Yes."

"Why do you?"

"Because God gave it to me!" She clapped her hands at the thought of it.

"That is right. Why did He give it to you?"

"Because I believe in Jesus!"

One afternoon she was too excited to concentrate, and the reading stopped entirely while she told us the news. A Spanish-speaking man, an educated man, had asked her father for permission to marry her. Her father had not given his answer yet, but it was apparent that Amalia was thrilled at the prospects—he was a good catch according to their standards.

There was one thing that made her father hesitate about his answer. The man was already married. His wife had left him, but because he was sure that she was not coming back, he wanted another one. Amalia asked us our opinion. Was it right to marry a man who already had a wife? We told her that God did not like it, but she interrupted us with the news that the suitor had said they would be forgiven. He would take the matter direct to the pope if necessary. It was apparent that his words had a more exciting ring than ours.

A few days later while Amalia and her mother Luisa were visiting us, Catarina came in and told us that two gentlemen were outside and wanted to speak to us. That was a courteous thing to do. Instead of appearing as strange men on our doorstep, they had contacted a mutual friend, Catarina, and had asked her to announce their visit. Of course we said, "Let them come in."

Well, they did not even have one foot inside before Amalia and Luisa had jumped up with, "We must be going." The four of them met at the door, and with considerable confusion we tried to bid one couple good-bye at the same time we bid the others welcome. That would not have been difficult except that those guests could not seem to pass each other. If, as their formality would have it to appear, they were strangers, what had caused them to forget the existence of Florrie and me? The women bade us good-bye and the men greeted us with mechanical phrases and expressionless faces. I was still puzzled when the seemingly impossible was accomplished, and the women were out and the men in.

Once the women had gone, the conduct of the men seemed so normal and businesslike that I wondered if I had been imagining things. The sister of one of the men was sick and they had come to ask for medicine and, if we were willing, to escort us to the girl's home. We went and helped the girl as best we could.

The next day Amalia was down to see us again, but every mention of the visit brought forth giggles. At last the story came out. She was so "embarrassed" and "ashamed." One of the men was the one who was asking to marry her, and the other was the go-between. Here in our house they had accidentally met. Amalia covered her face in shame and giggled with delight as she said it.

The lesson that day was the last Amalia had. Her father gave his consent to the marriage, and Amalia did not come back to the house again. According to custom, once the father had accepted money from the bridegroom, thus sealing the engagement, the girl was closely chaperoned. She seldom left home, and then only in the presence of her mother.

Florrie and I were sorry that the engagement had gone through. Aside from the complications of his wife, we hated to see Amalia leave Chalco to go to her husband's village. She had enjoyed the Bible studies and we were disappointed that they must stop so soon.

It was about two months later that Florrie and I awoke to the sound of a dance orchestra. When we were dressed and could inquire of Catarina, we learned that it was Amalia's wedding music. Because of the complications, the parents were substituting an elaborate wedding for the usual marriage ceremony. The music which we heard was to go on for most of twenty-four hours while the guests danced and feasted. As a special feature, eighty guests signed as witnesses to the marriage. The number of witnesses added prestige to the parents, for not everybody could assemble eighty people with the ability to sign their names. The witnesses were increased beyond their usual number because the marriage was considered risky, and the witnesses were a warning to the groom to be on his best behavior. If anything happened to the bride, theoretically those witnesses were ready to take him to task.

Florrie and I hoped that we would not be invited to the wedding. We liked Amalia, and we even liked the little we knew of the groom, but we did not see how we could go to the wedding and by our presence sanction his taking on a second wife. In Chalco guests were frequently invited as a party began, but as the morning wore on and more and more people passed on their way to the wedding, we relaxed. We thought that it was now too late for an invitation even to a Mazatec party.

But no sooner had we reached that conclusion than we saw Luisa standing in the doorway in her beautiful fiesta finery. Hardly was she seated before she invited us to the wedding. Perhaps we could have made the excuse that we were too busy, but she knew that for friends business could stop. Such an excuse might make her angrier than if we told her the truth. We had decided that if we were invited we would either go and say nothing, or we would stay home and tell them why. The more we had thought about it, the more we knew that we could not go. We had talked so much about Jesus Christ that people had come to connect us with Him. We felt that for us to go to such a wedding would be to shame Him.

As gently as we could, we told Luisa that we could not go. We could not because we did not think it right for a man to marry another woman when he was already married to one. We didn't say more. We did not need to, for we had told Amalia before their engagement how we felt. But even with that one quiet statement Luisa broke into tears. She thought it was wrong too, but it was not her fault. It was her husband who had insisted on the arrangements. "It is the man," she said, "who rules."

By that time, if not before, our own eyes were full of tears. We changed the subject to say what a fine girl Amalia was, and that we hoped she would be happy in her new home.

Luisa straightened, and with expressionless face, her head held high, she went back to be hostess of the biggest and gayest wedding of the season. As we bid her good-bye at the door, I looked beyond her and saw Marcos hoeing corn just outside. He saw the tears in our eyes, and an expression of wonder and sympathy came over his usually hard face. We turned, closing the door and window shutters, embarrassed to have been caught unhappy.

CHAPTER V

Whistle-Talk

(FALL OF 1940)

THINGS THAT WERE other people's excuses for not reading never seemed to happen to Inés. At least they never kept her from her lesson. Actually her lessons were a help to us too. While she was practicing her reading, we were learning about the tone of Mazatec. Because she read slowly, we could hear the pitch of the words more easily than we could in conversation.

Mazatec is one of those languages in which pitch makes a difference, a "tone language." Of course even in English, tone can change a compliment into a sneer, but by changing the tone in Mazatec the meaning of a word may change all the way from "water" to "cactus," or from "his trousers" to "his leaf."

Each syllable may be said on one of four basic pitches, or on a sequence of those pitches. The relationship of the four, one to another, remains the same, but the exact pitch varies depending on who is speaking (a man or a woman), and they vary somewhat according to the mood of the speaker. (Was she angry? Was she sleepy?)

We found the tone to be difficult and, even with

Inés' help, it seemed to hold us back. It took us considerable time to determine the correct tone for each word. We thought that if we could ignore it our work would go faster. We wondered if, in reading the translation, the people could guess the tone even when it was not written.

One day because we were questioning their value, we left the tone marks off the material we were using for Inés' lesson. She still read, but a little more slowly than usual. When she had finished, we asked her, "Which do you prefer? Do you like to read the page as it is now, or is it better when we write the tone marks?"

"It is better," answered Inés, "with the tone marks, because without them I can't tell whether it is saying, 'I can' or 'I will be able.'" Just that quickly she had picked out a pair of words that could be distinguished only by tone. Florrie and I knew that such a pair was just one of many, and if Inés needed help with that one, she would need it with the others.

It really was not strange that she wanted the tones indicated, since all Mazatecs were aware that each phrase of their language had rhythmical tune. In fact, it seemed so obvious to them that they never thought of telling anyone. We had to discover for ourselves why Tomás didn't answer when Catarina called. Instead he whistled sharply, starting high and loud, and ending softly on a lower pitch. Catarina didn't seem to mind. She gave him her instructions and he obeyed, going home for dinner, or to the market on an errand.

It was not just Tomás who whistled. When boys

were playing marbles in our yard, if one of them saw another on the road below, he whistled at him. The boy whistled back and sometimes he came up and joined the game. We were surprised that not a word was said, the newcomer merely started to play.

I do not remember when we first realized that in those situations the boys had actually been talking, but that they had talked, not with speech, but with whistles. The message had been conveyed by whistling the lilt of a spoken phrase.

As soon as Florrie and I knew that there was such a thing as whistle-talk, we wanted to understand it. Ida, Marta's cousin, was enthusiastic about teaching us. She whistled a message and told me to repeat it, but that part of my childhood had been neglected—I had never learned to whistle. Ida was amazed. Most Mazatecs, the men at least, learn so young that the lack of a whistle is almost as astonishing to them as lack of vocalization is to us. The only thing that saved me from being completely outclassed was the fact that in Mazatec culture women were not supposed to whistle. They understood the men's whistle-talk, but unless they were tomboys they responded verbally.

Ida was a tomboy, and she was not the least bit ashamed of whistling. With her help we learned to recognize and approximate, "Come here," "What do you want?" and a few other frequently used expressions. Much of her teaching was done while we were walking, and I did pretty well on the level part of the trail, but after we had climbed a little while, I quit trying. Ever-impatient Ida wanted to

know why. I told her that I had not any breath.
She chuckled and turned to her friend. "Poor thing.
She left her breath down the path. Go down and get
it for her."

She would never permit any silence to creep up
on us. If I wanted to whistle that was fine, but if
not she was always ready with a question. Typical
were, "How deep is the ocean? Is it over a horse's
head?" and, "Which is nearer—Russia or Guada-
lajara?" Or perhaps it was, "Why do you have
black hair?"

She was not the only one who asked that. Florrie's
hair was blond and that seemed to fit a light com-
plexion, but apparently black hair above my white
face looked queer. Anyway they ignored it and
named us according to our skins, that is, they called
us "the white-headed women."

That was the expression the men whistled when
they announced our approach and we heard it so
frequently that eventually it attracted our attention
almost as quickly as the spoken phrase would have
done.

Once we were conscious that their whistling conveyed a message, we frequently guessed what the
message was by watching the reaction to it. When
Esteban and Marcos were hoeing together, Esteban
usually whistled his orders and if they were working
in the field in front of our house, we could see him
respond. We could also hear some of the older boys
in the neighborhood as they whistled their arrangements for going for firewood together.

Even after we knew that whistle-talk existed, however, it was easy for me to overlook it and to con-

sider it as the noise of a lighthearted boy. There was the day that Inés was talking with us while Marcos stood in our doorway. He was whistling but not loudly enough to send a message very far, and I ignored him. To me, his whistle was just background noise. Then I noticed that Inés was vexed, and Marcos' twinkling eyes made me suspect that she had reason. "What's the matter?" I asked her.

"He's calling me a man and telling me to go for firewood!"

Marcos whistled again, and this time I noticed the slow precision of it and recognized it as whistle-talk. Inés turned toward him with a glint in her eye and Marcos fled.

As time went on I became aware of the difference between a whistled song and whistle-talk. A whistled song was smooth, almost continuous, whereas whistle-talk was punctuated with pauses. The number of pitches in song was indefinite, but in whistle-talk they were limited. Whistle-talk also seemed slower and more stately than music. As those differences became apparent to me, I grew more alert to the whistle-talk and sometimes when I did not understand, I would ask someone to put the message into spoken words.

CHAPTER VI

Friendliness

(FALL OF 1940)

THE MAZATECS liked to go visiting, and they liked to be around when others did. They were especially interested when folks came to our house. They not only kept tabs on the medical work, but they gleaned village news from the patients. Catarina had the habit of dropping whatever she was doing and slipping in whenever she saw someone new at our door. I could not see that it bothered the patients; in fact, some of them felt more at ease with one of their own people around. Probably infected sores were the thing we treated most frequently, but earaches were prevalent that winter too, and a number of women brought babies with draining ears.

When I worked on a baby, I jabbered at it continually. I used to speak to it in Mazatec but it confused the mother and she would interrupt to apologize for the baby's silence. "He's just a little baby; he does not talk yet."

But I could speak in English undisturbed, and so I did. Or sometimes I did not talk a language, but if the baby said, "Waaa," I said, "Waaa," back to it. And when it said, "Oooo," I said, "Oooo." The babies seemed to enjoy it and so did I.

The neighbor women who watched most frequently decided that all babies before they learned Mazatec spoke English. "No," Florrie and I told them.

"Yes," they insisted. "Eunice and the babies sound just alike. She can talk to them, but we cannot."

"All babies," we told them, "make the same kind of noises no matter what country they are in."

"That is what we said! They talk English." Our telling them otherwise did no good; after all, they had heard me talk and the baby respond, and they had heard the baby coo and me respond. Seeing was believing.

Probably it was just as well when the subject changed to the apron I was wearing. It was a plastic apron, and one of the women asked me what it was called. I was always startled when they asked me the name for something in Mazatec. I was the one who was trying to learn their language, and it had not occurred to me that I could teach them any of it. I answered with a word I thought appropriate, *apron*.

"Is that cloth?" asked one of the women and felt it. Then I remembered that the parts that made up the word apron meant, "cloth-put-against." No, it was not cloth—so what should it be called? The women discussed the problem. First they wanted to know what it was actually made of. They did not have a word for *plastic,* so the best I could do was to tell them that it was something like *rubber*— the word they used when describing any waterproof material. The women tried out the combination "rubber-put-against" but they rejected it. Finally, a bit hesitatingly, they agreed on "cloth-put-against-which-is-rubber," that is, a "rubber apron." That little incident helped me to see that original meaning of word parts (like *cloth*) can be lost when the broader meaning of the compound has become well established. Little hints like that helped me to be patient with visitors—I was constantly learning from them—and encouraged me to go calling.

When the Mazatecs were feeling friendly, they made good hostesses in little ways never thought of by Emily Post. There was the day my hostess insisted on moving my chair. When she saw that I did not understand why, she explained simply, "You might get wet if you sit there." That remark perplexed me more than ever, so she pointed to the thatched roof overhead. "You were sitting under the pole where the rats run." Of course! Then I understood. There were no cellars in Chalco, no attic, no double walls, and at least in the daytime that restricted the rats to the roof. They hid in the sugarcane leaves and ran up and down the rafters and supporting frame. I thanked my hostess for her thoughtfulness and hoped that if the time ever came I would do as well by my guests. So far we had not had much rat trouble. We had a rat trap and by using it more or less constantly we managed to keep our roof unoccupied.

Florrie and I had found a snake in the house one time, but it was not a poisonous one. Catarina had muttered that the snake's entrance had been the fault of our wooden floor. They never had snakes in their house, she said. Florrie and I decided that she was right. The floor was about six inches above the ground and the dark, damp space in between made a nice den for insects and animals. Because the space was inaccessible to us, we had no way of cleaning them out. Esteban had put in that floor because we had asked him to. Now experience had taught us that the original dirt one would have been better. The soil in Chalco was damp clay, and when it was packed down hard, it seemed cleaner than our wooden floor which had wide cracks between it and the wall.

To the Mazatecs, the greatest advantage in our wooden floor was its warmth—it was not so cold to sleep on as a damp clay one. The wooden floor was also appreciated by barefoot women, since the continual cold and dampness of a dirt one sometimes caused cracks in the soles of their feet. Some of them, like Catarina, found comfort in a chip of wood. She kept it by her chair and rested her feet on it whenever she sat sewing.

People who could afford it slept on a bed, and although the bed was without mattress or springs, the wooden frame did the important thing of keeping them off the ground. Probably every Mazatec knew what it was like to sleep on the ground, for even if their family possessed a bed, whenever company came either they or their company had to sleep on the floor. Most houses were crowded during the last days of October and the first ones of November, for that was when relatives gathered to celebrate All Saints' Day.

The celebration seemed to be the most joyful time of the year. An air of excitement prevailed as families worked together decorating an altar. Their attitude reminded me of a family in the States decorating a Christmas tree.

The women scrubbed up a table and washed and ironed a cloth with which to cover it. The men brought small banana trees, or branches from some other tree, to make an arch over it. The children brought oranges, picked with a stem and leaves because "it is prettier that way." Bread baked in the shape of men, flowers, fruit, and special delicacies was arranged around candles and a sacred picture.

The celebration began on October 31, when candles were burned beside the graves of dead children. On the next day, November 1, candles were burned beside the graves of the adults. Except for the sick, and for one member of each household who was left guarding the home, the whole village went to the cemetery.

The fact that they were in a cemetery did not depress the people; rather, in a holiday spirit, they visited with those standing around the surrounding graves. They were conscious of the beauty of thousands of candles burning against the background of brown earth and surrounded by men in sparkling white trousers and women in embroidered dresses.

When the weather was nice they had a wonderful time, but even if the celebration fell on a rainy or windy day, they still burned candles beside the graves. If it was raining, not as many people went to the cemetery, but some from each family were selected to keep the candles burning.

For the Mazatecs, burning a candle beside a grave on All Saints' Day was a way of helping the dead one. They said that the burning candle was food; in fact, they said that it was his *tortilla,* and that a burning candle was as important to the dead as *tortillas* were to the living.

Some people put as many as twenty down the center of the grave, considering that the amount of food each dead one received was in proportion to the number of candles that were burned on his grave.

To keep the candles burning in bad weather people shielded them from the wind with their blankets or shawls. Some cupped the flame in their hands to keep it from being extinguished by the rain.

But even if the weather was pleasant and the people were out in all their finery, the scene was still heartrending to Florrie and me. The people loved their departed folks, but the way they were trying to help them was futile. If their loved ones had depended on the Lord, they didn't need burning candles or any other type of food—they already had everything they needed. Jesus had said: "I am the bread of life: he that cometh to me shall never hunger; and he that believeth on me shall never thirst" (John 6:35). But in their very burning of the candles they were demonstrating that they themselves were not counting on Jesus to feed their loved ones, and in their lack of belief they were "condemned already" to be like the one who begged that Lazarus might dip the tip of his finger in water and cool his tongue with it. These poor people were substituting a feeble candle for the glorious promises of God.

On November 2, the people took the food that

was left on their altars and cooked more for the purpose of exchanging goodies with their friends and neighbors. Florrie and I were pleased to be included in their friendship, but as the gifts were showered upon us, we thought of I Corinthians 8. Did that chapter apply to our situation? "As concerning therefore the eating of those things that are offered in sacrifice unto idols. . . . But meat commendeth us not to God: for neither, if we eat, are we the better; neither, if we eat not, are we the worse. But take heed lest by any means this liberty of yours become a stumblingblock to them that are weak." The exchange of gifts from off the altar seemed so wholehearted and friendly that we hated to sound a sour note unless it was necessary. After considerable thought we decided that for the time being we would eat and say nothing.

On the morning of November 2, Florrie and I threw out the breakfast which we ourselves had prepared and ate instead the bananas, oranges, and tamales which had been brought as a gift. Then Catarina sent over word that we were not to cook a dinner because she would supply us, and Tomas, as excited as a boy with a Christmas secret, whispered that she was cooking chicken and chili sauce.

At one o'clock we started the fire and put on water for the tea we expected to drink with Catarina's dinner. Then there was a knock at the door and a servant of a well-to-do storekeeper, Mrs. Sánchez, handed us a basket filled with steaming hot food. We thanked him for it and, because Catarina and the whole family would be disappointed if they knew that someone else had brought us the traditional fiesta dish, we scooted it out of sight as soon as he had gone. Then we waited.

An hour later we drank our tea. Still later Catarina appeared at the window. "I was going to bring over your dinner, but when I saw what the other people had sent you, I decided to give you mine tomorrow."

As soon as Catarina was out of sight we chuckled. We might have known that no one could get into our house without her seeing him. As we heated up the food sent by Mrs. Sánchez, we admitted to ourselves that we had not yet learned to predict our neighbors' actions, and we wondered if we ever would.

CHAPTER VII

A Milestone

(SPRING OF 1941)

"I HAVE NOT DONE a speck of work today!" I told Florrie as we got up from the supper table. She just looked at me. Well . . . it is true that I had reviewed Tomás on his Bible verses—he could recite about forty different ones. I had taught Catarina a new one, that made twenty for her now. I had showed our English walnut to several different people after treating their medical needs.

That was a very special walnut. The meat had been taken from the shell and a ribbon had been substituted. The ribbon was made up of four sections, each section a different color. As I pulled the end, the people watched the ribbon emerge and listened as I used the color as an illustration. The black stood for our hearts full of sin; the red was for the blood of Christ, the ransom price by which we can be freed from the death penalty; white was for the condition of our hearts after they had been cleansed by Christ; and gold was for Heaven, the home of those who had been given eternal life.

I liked to tell that story, especially when the people reacted as one man had done. He had interrupted me to go to the door and call his friend. Together they had listened while the story was re-

peated. Then to each other they commented softly,
"It is the truth that she is telling."

Responses like that were our recompense for language work, but if the day was so full of people that
I did not get some studying done, I felt that the·
day was lacking. At that time I was trying to write
a sketch of as much as I knew of Mazatec grammar.
Writing it helped show up the gaps in my knowledge and once I knew where I was lacking, I could
ask my informant for specific sentences that would
fill in that lack. We needed all the grammar we
could figure out if we were going to make a good
translation. A good translation could not be made
with just "words," those words had to be tied
together with correct grammar signals and in the
correct order.

Every once in awhile our bad grammar tripped us
up. That is what it did in John 5:22: "For the
Father judgeth no man, but hath committed all
judgment unto the Son." Now, Christ does take
the punishment for those who trust Him as Saviour,
and acknowledge Him as Lord, but that was not
what was intended by John 5:22. We certainly
needed to know more grammar.

But we needed more than grammar, and more
than words. We needed to know any connotations
that went with the words. "He is crazy!" children
said. "You are crazy!" they said to each other.
There was no question about the basic meaning
of the phrase, but we decided that it would not do
for John 10:20: "And many of them said, He hath
a devil, and is mad." The word seemed to be slang—
not dignified enough for the Word of God.

We even needed to know indelicate words. Specifically we needed to know the word for "adultery," but Catarina figured that there were certain words that we as single girls should not hear and did not need to know and she refused to tell us. We explained to her that the word occurred in the Bible and that we were trying to put in writing everything the Bible said, but her mind was made up, and except for a grunt she remained silent.

We did not want to ask just anybody; Catarina's reaction had made us self-conscious. We did ask Mrs. Sánchez but her answer—"he goes around with her" or "he lives with her"—was not specific enough. Certainly the Bible should not be made to say, "Thou shalt not live with a woman." Nor would that phrase do for the verse Florrie was concerned about. "They say unto him, Master, this woman was taken in adultery, in the very act" (John 8:4).

A few days later an American anthropologist and his wife came to Chalco. They were lovely folks and glad to be helpful. We told them our difficulty and requested that the anthropologist get the word for "adultery" from some of the men—they would not have the reticence of Catarina. "Sure!" he said. "I'll find out for you."

We do not know whom he asked, but he inquired and was given a word that he thought we might use for "to commit adultery." The next time he and his wife visited us, he handed it to us written on a piece of paper.

We use no words in the translation without checking them with someone other than the person from whom we first heard them. It happened that

Marta came over the day we decided to check that one.

"Marta," Florrie said, "tell me what this word means," and she read the word which the anthropologist had given us. For a second or two Marta looked at her in blank amazement. Then she hid her face in her hands and shrieked with laughter. Between her fingers we could see tears running down her red face. We had known that the word would be a hard one to explain, but we had not expected that much reaction. "Marta," Florrie spoke gently, trying to quiet her. But Marta would not be soothed. When she finally got control of herself she was belligerent. "Who told you that word?"

We were not going to give the anthropologist away, after all we had asked him to get it for us. We refused to say where we had learned it. "Who told you that word?" Marta demanded again. Instead of answering we asked, "What does it mean?" She pushed us aside and went to the yard. "Catarina!" she called loudly.

Catarina was right there, waiting to find out what the rumpus was about. We did not hear what Marta said to her, but we heard Catarina's loud denial. "I didn't! I teach them only good words!" and she half-accused Marta of having taught us herself. Loudly Marta protested. Children gathered to see what was going on, and as I watched the two so vehement in the accusations, I wondered too where it would end. But they managed to convince each other that someone else had been guilty, and they came back to us. Marta now was beyond laughter.

"Don't ever say that word again!" she ordered; and Catarina supported her with, "It was a bad person who told you that word."

We had no desire to use it. We wanted a word which could be read aloud in a public meeting, and any word which caused as violent a reaction as that one had done would disrupt rather than help a meeting. We went back to a polite paraphrase for John 8:4.

Florrie's main concern those days was to have something with which to complete the first draft of the New Testament. She felt that the end was in sight and she was turning all her energies into reaching that milestone. There were not enough hours in the day for her, so her evenings became longer and longer. I thought my own evenings were long enough, for I went to bed at eleven, but I was usually asleep before she put down her pen.

Because we were driving toward a specific goal, we left the house only when it was necessary, but Catarina succeeded in getting us out one day. She took us down to see a nephew of hers who had tuberculosis. He was coughing and pus was draining from two holes near his collar bone, and from three more just under his chin. I knew of no way of helping him permanently, but the sores would be less objectionable if they were washed off with hydrogen peroxide occasionally. When I suggested it to the mother, she was not enthusiastic, for she had already tried hydrogen peroxide. I tried not to encourage her, but Catarina told enthusiastically of the children who came to the house with sores on their legs, how I treated them, and how quickly they healed. "Ah!" said the family, and they discussed the matter. "Some people have healing hands. We can use the same medicine as they do, but it does no good," and they told tales illustrating the point. "It isn't the medicine at all! It's her hands that heal," they decided. After more discussion they turned back to me. Humbly they apologized and explained, "We know you are busy, but the boy is thin; he cannot get much thinner without dying. Please come and put medicine on yourself."

Sometimes sores, which had not healed for them, healed when I treated them, because I cleaned the pus away before applying the medicine, but I could not do that for those sinuses. As I hesitated, they repeated their request, and I could not turn down a plea like that. I went back. The boy did not get better, but through my visits the family learned about Christ and to sing a hymn or two.

In the meantime, Florrie had started work on the Gospel of Matthew. I watched her progress through that book more closely than I had any of the others, because that was the book which had been left until last, and when it was finished, the first draft of the entire New Testament would be finished.

When she reached chapter 11, we wondered if a Mazatec might not understand verses 28 and 30 of that chapter even more easily than people at home. "Come unto me, all ye that labor and are heavy laden. . . . My yoke is easy and my burden is light." Most Mazatecs from the time they are little are expected to carry their share of physical burdens. They use a long rope with a wide band in the middle section. The ends of the rope are tied around the pack to be carried, the band is placed across the top of the carrier's head, and the pack hangs down his back from the top of his head.

Mazatecs are very conscious of the difference between a "bad burden" and a "good burden." Bad burdens have sharp edges which cut into their backs, or moving parts which tend to throw them off balance as they walk. A good burden is light and shaped to their backs.

Esteban, like most men, had to carry firewood on his back. After carrying it up the mountain, he was so glad to get rid of it that he never lifted it down. He tossed his head, the rope came off, and the pack hit the ground. Even though we were inside the house, Florrie and I knew when he had arrived by the thud with which the pack landed. We could also hear Esteban's whistled sigh of relief which almost invariably followed his release from the burden.

Florrie and I remembered Esteban and his firewood when we read the verse: "My yoke is easy and my burden is light." Perhaps, at least for the time being, we could translate *yoke* with the Mazatec term for "carrying rope."

Day by day more and more verses were done and 3 by 5 slips on which they were written stretched longer and longer behind the Matthew index card. Then on April 26, 1941, the slip with Matthew 28:20 was placed there, and at that moment the first draft of the Mazatec New Testament was done.

CHAPTER VIII

At the Summer Institute of Linguistics

(SUMMER OF 1941)

WE DID NOT CELEBRATE the finish of that first draft, perhaps because we knew that this was only the beginning—many revisions lay ahead of us. Perhaps we did not celebrate because we were too busy closing up the house and getting ready to leave for the summer.

Mr. W. C. Townsend, the director of Wycliffe Bible Translators, had asked me to help at the Summer Institute of Linguistics in Sulphur Springs, Arkansas. I had helped the previous summer too, and I had been amazed (most nurses would have been), when asked to teach phonetics.

My struggles with Mazatec had been my training ground, and my brother Ken had briefed and tutored me further. He had been translating the New Testament for the Mixtec tribe and most of his letters to me from there contained bits of linguistic advice. In one letter he would advise me about tone in language, and the next letter would have an outline of the way words and sentences are made up.

When it came to teaching, Ken told me to give the students dictation of sounds found in non-English languages. He was sure I would not be fast enough to think up drill material on my feet, so he warned me to prepare lists of foreign words and of nonsense syllables in advance. Having the material written out helped, but it took more than that. I had to practice pronouncing the combinations until I could make my lips, tongue, uvula, and vocal cords act either as a team, or independently one from the other.

I kept a copy of my work and as I started back for the second summer, I was expecting an easier time. I knew that class preparation wouldn't be hard, but even so I was concerned when my arrival was delayed until the evening before classes were to start.

Arriving about supper time, I went directly to the dining hall and was immediately surrounded by other staff members. Their greeting, "Oh, Eunice, are we ever glad to see you!" had something ominous about it, but I didn't have long to wonder. The one in charge pushed through and shook my hand. "Very glad to see you. We are counting on you to teach four hours of phonemics tomorrow."

I thought he was joking and answered him in that manner, but the others shouted, "That is the truth! Ken's not here." I did not believe them. Evie, his wife, was there—but she came in from California. Ken was coming from Michigan. I still doubted, but I glanced at Evie. Almost imperceptibly she nodded and I knew it was so.

The words of the joking staff swirled around my head. Tomorrow. Four hours. I had never taught phonemics. It was phonetics I taught. Where was the preparation time? It was already six o'clock. I had to eat, find something to wear, and be ready for class by eight in the morning.

I considered the other staff members who were there; perhaps one of them could start the classes. Almost immediately I dropped the idea, for, except for the one teaching grammar, I had had more experience than they, and I had also listened while Ken talked about the linguistic literature and his own ideas about language.

Perhaps the students could be started off with grammar. But it was thought that the students understood grammar more easily if they had a little background in phonemics (a study of alphabets). Ken had agreed to give them four hours a day in phonetics and phonemics the first week. The grammar classes were not scheduled to start until the second week. Ken must have remembered the agreement when he sent his telegram. Addressed to me it said, "Sorry, Sis. Held up here. Take over until I arrive." Probably he had chosen the only way. For better or for worse the job was up to me.

Evie helped. She pressed a dress for me, saw to it that my bed had sheets, and kept people away so that I could study. The job wasn't an impossible one because I had sat in on Ken's classes the previous year; I knew his goals and what he considered basic. But it took me until three in the morning before I was satisfied that I had the material under control.

At 8 A.M. I stood in front of the student body. They knew I was substituting, but they were friendly and willing that I should prove acceptable. Forty faces all looking my direction made my heart pound, but by the end of the first hour I knew I had won. The students were learning, and if Ken did not delay too long, everything would be all right.

A telegram that afternoon told how long the delay would be. He would arrive the next day at 2 P.M. I would have to teach three morning hours, but he could take the fourth hour in the afternoon. Preparation was easier that evening, for I knew that I had material enough to keep the students profitably occupied.

Ken came and a load rolled off my shoulders. When people asked him why he was delayed he answered, "It was in connection with my dissertation." He had been studying at the University of Michigan and the dissertation was the one required for fulfillment of a Ph.D. degree.

That answer satisfied most everyone, but Evie knew that he had expected to be on time, so when we were alone she asked again, "What happened?"

He protested, laughed, then told us.

He had been determined to get the dissertation finished and turned in before leaving Michigan. He was a poor typist and time was running short. He had to hire a steno, and another, and another. They made the deadline, but by the time the dissertation was done, he did not have enough money left to buy a ticket to Arkansas. He had not been late from choice—he couldn't come.

When he saw that the classes had gone well, he was convinced that the inconvenience had really been due to the goodness of the Lord. Because he had been short of funds, he had arrived late. Because of his late arrival I had taught phonemics, and it was good I had done so. It speeded the growth and development of staff. The Lord knew how fast our staff needed to grow, and, but for the emergency, responsibilities would have been delegated much more slowly.

The Lord knew that the very next year the Summer Institute of Linguistics classes would move to the campus of the University of Oklahoma. He knew that by 1957 there would be branch schools at the University of North Dakota, in Canada, Australia, and England, and that about 500 students would receive help from them each year.

Just because He had withheld a little money, I had been thrown into the job, making the way for others to follow. That year Evie taught phonetics, and all of us took a hand in tutoring phonemics. With a common purpose we worked together to help the students. All of them expected to go to some foreign country: Brazil, Guatemala, China, Nigeria, India, Mexico. Most of them would live among a people who spoke an unanalyzed language, and many of them would be translating the Bible for that people.

Most of the staff had been working with an Indian tribe, but they had come back for the summer because they felt that it was worth delaying the translation on which they themselves were working, in order that the students might be better prepared to translate for still other tribes. They taught with a fervor, and the students studied with a fervor born of the conviction that a knowledge of linguistics was basic to Bible translation.

CHAPTER IX

Something in Print

(FALL OF 1941)

WHILE I WAS IN THE STATES teaching, Florrie
stayed in Mexico City. At that time there were
about twenty-five other members of the Wycliffe
Bible Translators who were also working in tribes,
and someone was needed who could forward mail
and change dollars into Mexican money and send it
on to those in small towns. Florrie handled some
of their city business and at the same time took a
course or two at the University of Mexico.

Her studies and work as secretary kept her busy,
but she took time to check and recheck seven Bible
verses which she had previously translated into
Mazatec. Satisfied that they were done to the best
of her ability, she had them printed in the form of
a small leaflet. It was just one sheet of paper folded
in half, and on one side the verses were in Mazatec,
and on the other the same verses were in Spanish.

She received the proof of the leaflet just a day or
two after I got back to Mexico City from the States.
Both of us went over it and made corrections before
returning it to the printer, but when we received
the finished copies, we found that two words were
misspelled. Even though we had the excuse that

Mazatec, like any foreign language, was hard to proofread, we were ashamed at overlooking two errors in seven verses.

One of the reasons for printing the leaflet had been to gain experience on something less expensive than a Gospel, but we had not anticipated that the first thing it would teach us was to be more careful in our proofreading.

We expected to use it in testing our alphabet. We wanted to see if the people would accept our choice of letters. The reaction of those who had been to school and read Spanish was especially important. In Mazatec culture anyone who had reached the third or fourth grade was highly educated, and their opinion carried considerable weight with the others. If they disapproved of the alphabet, the less educated, afraid of ridicule, would not read it.

We hoped they would accept the alphabet and that the people would read the leaflet. As we looked at the little leaflet, we daydreamed—we saw parents teaching their children about Christ, and numbers of them meeting together to learn of Him. We saw the standard of living rise as drunkenness and crime decreased and energies were turned to honest work. It was just a little leaflet, only seven verses, but if the Lord blessed it, it would at least be a beginning. Small as it was, something was in print at last, and we were eager to return with it to the tribe.

When we traveled in to Chalco, we left most of our baggage with a mule driver to bring in two days later. That is, the arrangements were that he would bring it two days later. Experience had taught us that things did not always turn out as we had planned. We took no chance on the leaflets being delayed. We carried them with us, tied to the saddle in a bag along with our lunch, toothbrushes, and a change of shoes.

As soon as the Chalco people saw us, they asked, "What did you bring new?" Other years we had shown them the victrola, our portable radio, or a magazine with pictures. This year we took out the leaflet and said, "Look at this!" Everyone was interested and a little proud. They considered their language to be inferior, partly because there were no books in it. Occasionally a Spanish-speaking teacher had tried to write it, had failed, and had told the people that their language was so poor that it could not be written. When the people saw the leaflet, even those who could not read recognized it as being similar to "books," and it gave them a lift in morale.

Everyone wanted a copy, but we refused to sell them, and we gave them only to people who could read them, or who had memorized them. We knew that they would show them around, and if they were not able to read them, the leaflet might discourage rather than encourage readers.

Rivalry sprang up among the children of the village as they tried to "win the paper." They could not memorize all the verses at one time, so they came back and learned a verse or two a day until they had completed the seven. When the paper was theirs, most of them thanked us and sat politely for a moment. Then after the customary, "I am going now," they touched their fingertips to ours in a proper Mazatec handshake and left. Once they were out the door, restraint was gone and they dashed down the path, hurrying to show off their prize.

Some of the women considered themselves incapable of either reading or memorizing, and even when we read the verses to them, many responded with a bored "yes" every time we paused for breath. Those who took their social duties more seriously varied their response with, "That is so." One woman, however, made up for a hundred "that-is-so-ers." She thanked us by saying, "I am an old woman, but in all these years only you have told me these things."

The family of the boy with tuberculosis had that kind of interest. When I went to see him, I made it a habit of taking the leaflet, or an Old Testament Bible story with me. One day I had the story of Daniel in the Lions' Den, and the family gathered to listen while the father read it. When he read the edict that Daniel was to be thrown to the lions, he laid down the paper and the family sympathized with "poor Daniel," and they protested at the treatment he was receiving at the hands of "bad people." The father picked up the story again, and when he read Daniel's triumphant: "My God hath sent his angels and hath shut the lions' mouths," they exclaimed with delight, and the father summed it up with, "That is because he believed in God, I guess." Perhaps this family had understood quickly because I had read several other stories with them. I had noticed that people were apt to have trouble with their first story.

One day I gave the story of Daniel in the Lions'

Den to a teen-age girl. She read it aloud without too much difficulty, and when she had finished, I askèd her, "What was it about?" No answer. I tried again. "What did Daniel do?" Because I urged, she made a guess. "He hid in a pit so the lions would not eat him."

Her lack of understanding had not been the fault of the way the story was written, its vocabulary, or bad grammar. Perhaps it was because her schooling had been in Spanish, and reading for her was only an exercise in producing sequences of sounds— she had not thought of it as a means of gaining information.

Perhaps her lack of understanding was due to her basic beliefs. Biblical ideas were so new to her that even when she read the words correctly, she reinterpreted them until the resulting idea was in accord with tribal life. Whichever it was, her answer had made me realize that I was dependent on the Holy Spirit. If He didn't help the Mazatecs, they would never believe in Christ. But He would help. Quietly, with a prayer in my heart, we went back over the story again, and that time she understood.

Soon after that the Japanese attacked Pearl Harbor. Some of the merchants in Chalco heard of it on their radios, but several weeks passed before the news reached the poorer people. When they did hear, however, they wanted information whenever they could get it. Two young men who knew we had a radio wanted to ask us about the war, so they came down with a boy who often looked at magazines in our house.

We turned on the radio, and, while we waited for

a newscast, they asked questions. They wanted to know who was fighting, why they were fighting, who was going to win, and when they were going to win. We talked for awhile and then, as the news had not yet come on the radio, we changed the subject and told them that we had something to show them. They became concerned. "What are they going to do?" they murmured to ever-present Catarina.

"It is God's Word," she answered, and their friend added, "It tells us about eternal life."

The men didn't read it as easily as some had done, but they struggled through and became so interested that they forgot about the war. They read it over and over again, with Catarina, Tomás, and their friend coaching from the side lines. By half-memorizing, they read it smoothly enough so that they "won" and went away beaming.

Perhaps the most educated person to read the leaflet was a young man who had completed the sixth grade and had been teaching school ever since. We listened and watched carefully as he read, noticing on which words he hesitated and where he stumbled. The alphabet had thus far stood up before speakers with a slight knowledge of Spanish, and we wondered if it would pass this "educated" man. He hesitated at one of the letters not found in the Spanish alphabet, and we waited to see if he would reject the whole paper because of it. Instead he glanced at the Spanish translation on the opposite page, and by means of it he was able to guess the Mazatec.

He was still puzzled by the strange letter, however, so we told him other words containing it. As we listed them, understanding came over his face and he said, "That is the sound a Spanish person cannot pronounce." We agreed with his explanation, and he read on, satisfied that such a sound be written with a letter not in the Spanish alphabet. When he left, he took a leaflet with him, and as always we were glad that another bit of Scripture was in circulation, but we were glad too that the alphabet had passed one more test.

CHAPTER X

An Outsider

(FALL OF 1941)

WE HAD NOT EXPECTED the young teacher very soon, but it so happened that a new government nurse came to town. She heard about us and wanted to meet us, so he brought her up. She had been sent out by the government to help the people of Chalco. She was not the first one, but the others had not stayed long. They missed the activity of the city, the movies, and Spanish-speaking friends; then too without a knowledge of Mazatec they found it hard to buy in the market.

This woman was a widow with two children, and we hoped that her family responsibilities would make her more willing to forego pleasures of city life. We hoped she would stay awhile, so when we talked with her, we did not tell her that hardly a nurse before her had stayed more than six months; we just told her how glad we were that she had come, and invited her to visit us often.

She was enthusiastic about her job, but a bit nervous because she spoke only Spanish, and she knew that many of her patients would speak only Mazatec. She hoped that she could hire a boy for an interpreter.

A day or two later Catarina told us that Luisa, Amalia's mother, was ill. She also said that they had called the nurse and that she had given her an injection. Catarina did not think she was very ill, and we did not inquire into it any further. We knew that Luisa's family was one of the more progressive of the area and we were glad that they had called the nurse instead of a witch doctor.

The next morning as we were eating breakfast we heard a long quivering wail. We laid down our spoons and listened. The wail was joined by others until it was apparent that a whole family was weeping at once. "Luisa!" said Florrie. That was the answer. The wailing was an announcement of her death.

Women alone or in groups of two or three were soon on their way up to Luisa's house. Some were relatives who went to help prepare the funeral feast, and some were guests with flowers. About noon Florrie and I went too, and as we stepped into the house, Amalia threw herself into our arms with a cry of, "My mother is dead." We tried, not very successfully, to comfort her, and then we joined the guests at the other end of the room.

At each new arrival, the guests stopped talking to listen while Amalia greeted the newcomer. Then they picked up their conversation again. As at most funerals, the chief topic of conversation was the manner in which the person had died. This time the most often repeated phrase was, "The nurse did it!" Florrie and I disagreed, but we could not persuade anybody to our way of thinking. We were sure that the injection had not hurt Luisa, but the nurse had not been able to make herself understood by the family. They did not know what the medicine was, or what it was supposed to do, but the series of events, as they saw them, left them and their friends convinced that the medicine was at fault. According to them, soon after the nurse had given Luisa the injection, her condition became worse. She quit eating, and a few hours later she became—(that was a new word). For a minute the conversation buzzed on unheeded while I tried to figure it out. Its parts meant "dead-inside." It had been applied to Luisa when she was very ill, and had been followed by the sentence, "By morning she was dead." The word must mean "unconscious." (I mentally ran through my dictionary file. No, it was not there. I would add it later.)

Florrie and I did not stay long at the gathering. We sat a little while, drank a cup of coffee, and then went home. In the late afternoon we watched from our doorway as they took the body to the cemetery. They walked slowly, with the casket balanced on the shoulders of four men. Women carrying burning candles and white lilies preceded them, and men followed.

About a week later the nurse visited us again, and to our amazement she had come to say goodbye. She explained that she was leaving because she had been ill. The climate did not agree with her, she said. That sounded like the excuses I had heard before when other outsiders had left. We were disappointed, for we knew that the people needed help, so we urged her to stay longer. Her response was an emphatic, "No, I will not stay!"

Then she expressed amazement that we ourselves were staying. She for one could not bear to live among such barbarous people. "But we like them," we told her, "they are our friends."

"Friends? You are deceived." Then she told of the experience she had had. Nobody had notified her that Luisa had died, but, knowing that Luisa had been seriously ill, she had gone up in the afternoon to give her a second injection, and she had walked into the funeral gathering. One of Luisa's sons met her and he was drunk. When he saw the nurse, he cursed her and said, "You made my mother's children to suffer, now I'm going to make your children suffer!" Then he threw stones at her.

With bitterness the nurse told the incident, and she added, "You see? Some day you will wish you had not stayed." I was sorry. I wondered if I should have helped her more. Perhaps I should have told her that a Mazatec gave a separate invitation each time he wanted a witch doctor—or a nurse—to return. He didn't expect a nurse to come just because she knew the patient needed help. But that was just one custom that was different from hers. To feel at home, she would have to learn their language and become acquainted with many of their customs. As I listened to her tale I came to understand her week of illness. She had been genuinely ill, as a natural reaction to fear. I sympathized with her desire to leave; I would not have wanted to be that nurse, alone in a place like Chalco, but Florrie and I were not alone. We remembered to thank the Lord again that night for His constant protection.

CHAPTER XI

In the Mail at Last

(SPRING OF 1942)

As FLORRIE AND I deliberated over our knowledge of the Mazatec language and the work we had done on it, it seemed to us that the revision of the Gospel of John could be completed in the near future. All unrelated or unessential work was put aside as we turned our energies into finishing the task. For Florrie, language at that time appeared to be divided into two parts—one part composed of words found in John, and the other part composed of all other words. She was struggling and spending a large percentage of her waking moments to perfect the words of the one part, while she acquired information about the other part only as it happened to come to her attention. I marveled that she was able to pigeonhole even words common to religious terminology with a confident, "But that does not occur in John."

Part of her knowledge must have been built up by use of a checklist sent us by the American Bible Society. This list was made up of those words which are closely associated with Christian beliefs, such as *glorify, judge,* and *eternal.* Beside each word were the references indicating where it was found in the

Gospel of John. Its purpose was to promote consistency in the use of those words, for doctrines tend to build up around them as Bible teachers compare verse with verse. The rule of thumb was that one and only one Mazatec word should be used for each corresponding Greek word. If more than one word was used, it was with the knowledge that more were necessary to cover the area of meaning contained in the corresponding Greek term. The reverse was also true, for occasionally one Mazatec word covered two Greek terms.

The word *believe* was puzzling because an absolute Mazatec equivalent was lacking. To an English speaker, the Mazatecs seemed to be tangling the words *believe, hear,* and *obey.* A mother scolding her son might say, "Hear me!" at a time when an English-speaking mother would have said, "Obey me." When a child was slow in obeying, his mother might say, "Do you not believe?" The specific word *obey* in Mazatec included the idea of carrying something through to a finish. Such words required repeated checking before we could be sure of their meaning.

Sometimes Florrie felt that she had received all the help she could from our near neighbors, and she wanted to check certain words with someone who knew more Spanish. A slip of paper listing those words was almost always within her reach, and at every opportunity she questioned the more educated about them. From some people she received no help at all, from others she received only a little, but by combining all information she could come to a definite conclusion concerning each word.

Over a period of time she had noticed that the person most consistently helpful was Paula, one of the older Sánchez girls. She was married, widowed, and rearing two sons, and she seldom left her store, but whenever Florrie's list became long, we visited her. The three of us sat behind the counter and between those moments when Paula was wrapping up a piece of soap, or weighing out rice, she was answering Florrie's questions. Instead of telling us that two words were "the same," as other people frequently did, she contrasted them for us and helped us to understand by giving illustrations of their use.

But even Paula was ignorant of many of the words in the Spanish New Testament. Many times we could only define a word and ask her to put a name to that meaning. The Spanish word *parable* was one to which her only reaction was a puzzled look. But she was able to tell us that the "walking-word" which had been given us really meant "rumor," and "night-word" was "mystery." So we abandoned those words and once more we defined and explained the way in which Christ had used parables. Paula sat silent while we talked, and when we finished she asked quietly, "What about 'teaching-word'?" That seemed right, but we had never heard it before, certainly it was not a common word. Perhaps Paula had even made it up, but it paralleled "walking-word" and for the moment at least we were satisfied. Florrie's pencil moved down to the next item on her list.

Paula's help came from her patience and the intelligence with which she selected words. Her mother, Mrs. Sánchez, was also helpful but for a very different reason. She was highly impatient and frank in her dislike for any muddled sentences. Because of that very quality, we knew that if she had understood us, other people would understand too.

She had not been well, and because there was no doctor in town, she had gone to Mexico City for medical help. When she returned, she brought back a ten cc. vial of liver extract, and every other day she came to me for an injection of it. On January 6 she came just after three men dressed in bright silks and on horseback had led a parade down the main street. I asked her if she knew the origin of the celebration of the "three kings." She did not, so I told her about the three Wise Men and the Christmas star. She was amazed, and the pitch of her voice rose with her astonishment as she quizzed me, making sure that I had meant what I had said.

"The star moved across the sky?"

"Yes."

"And they followed it?"

"Yes."

"And that is how they found their way to Jesus?"

"Yes."

"What did they do in the daytime?" I almost jumped as she snapped that question, for I had never thought about that. Then she herself provided the answer from her own experience. "They must have traveled at night," she said, satisfied that people other than the Mazatecs knew how to avoid the hot sun.

Old Mrs. Sánchez did not have much interest in reading. Because of her eyes she did not even sew any more, but if I did not bring the subject up, she herself turned our conversation to religious things and asked me leading questions. Death was frequent in Chalco; babies died from pneumonia or dysentery, men died of violence, others died of tuberculosis. Perhaps because death was so close, Mrs. Sánchez liked to hear about Heaven and about how "God shall wipe away all tears from their eyes; and there shall be no more death, neither sorrow, nor crying." It was after our talk about that verse that she said, "I am old, I'll probably die first, then when you arrive I'll say, 'Hello, Eunice.'"

Florrie and I frequently wondered how many Mazatecs we would meet in Heaven. Of course we wanted to meet our near neighbors there, but we hoped there would also be some from the villages we could see in the distance, and from those out of sight beyond the mountain range. Some day maybe we could move out to those villages or make regular trips out to them, but in the meantime the medical work helped bring us in contact with strangers and people from other towns.

We used the opportunity to tell them about Christ, but we also used it as a check on the translation. We suspected that at times our neighbors understood us, not because we spoke accurately, but because they mentally compensated for our errors. Therefore before we could be satisfied with the translation, we needed to check it with people who were unaccustomed to our speech.

We made the most of the opportunity whenever a stranger came asking for medicine. Most frequently they wanted to have a wound or a sore treated. When I changed the dressing, I put a piece of newspaper on the floor and threw the old bandage on it. I had noticed that when people came for medicine they sat and talked until I had cleaned up whatever litter I had made for them. It seemed to be Mazatec etiquette to stay until I had disposed of the newspaper and had put the medicine away.

Well, some time before I cleaned it up I made it a habit of asking, "Do you know how to read?" If the patient said that he did not, I would tell him a Bible story. If he said, "I know a little bit," I was delighted.

"Good." I would tell him, "In a little while we will read in your language."

That frightened most of them and they would explain, "I cannot read my language; it is just Spanish that I can read."

"I will help you." And with that I picked up a few pages of the Gospel of John.

Perhaps I was taking advantage of them, but I learned to leave the medicine out so they would stay awhile. Then, in spite of their shyness, they would make an effort. Their innate politeness told them that they should at least try when I pointed to a piece of paper and said, "Read."

When they returned to have the wound dressed the second time, they read more easily, and of those who required several treatments, a number learned to enjoy reading, and several even returned for more after they were healed. We took their interest as an indication that the translation was acceptable, and we hoped that the current revision would be the final one.

If it were to be the final one, we needed to decide how to spell the names that occurred in the Bible. Some of them were already known to the people, but many were so strange that the Mazatecs did not even realize that they were names. There was no reason to expect them to pronounce them the English way, and they even had trouble with the customary Spanish pronunciation. We tried simplifying them enough to make them easily pronounceable by a Mazatec. We dropped final consonants— all Mazatec words end in a vowel. And if a name contained a difficult sequence of consonants, we left out one of them. But that idea did not work. We had to change back to the Spanish spelling. The people read the simplified names more easily, but they felt that names were Spanish and that to spell them any other way was wrong.

At the same time that we were experimenting with the spelling of the names, Florrie was checking the accuracy of the translation by comparing parallel passages. Until the references to those passages had been sent us by the American Bible Society, we had been almost unaware of the numerous phrases that were repeated throughout the Book of John, but once they were brought to our attention, we saw that we had translated the same phrase in various ways. Florrie spent days writing each translation beside its reference. Then when they were listed side by side, she chose the best one. The time was well spent, for although a phrase did not have to be translated exactly the same each time, it tended toward more accuracy to be aware of any differences. The way she worked at the task made me admire her. It seemed to me that the copying of the sentences on the list and the rephrasing of her rejected translations was a tedious job, but she never complained even though she worked late in the evenings to finish it. It was after seeing her spend every hour she could at the task, both during the day and in the evenings, that I remarked on her patience. Her response was with a look of surprise. "This does not take patience. I love it." That was a new idea to me, but I realized that it was probably so. Then she went on, "It is you who have patience while you are teaching those slow readers and putting up with the children."

Queer. I had not been conscious of any. Perhaps patience would have been required with little Rosalia if she had not been so closely associated with hope. She was a little girl of about six who frequently dropped in on her way to the market. We had the habit of teaching Bible verses to any of the children who came around, and so we were teaching her too. One morning I reviewed her on "Believe on the Lord Jesus Christ, and thou shalt be saved, and thy house," and then tried to teach her to sing "Jesus Loves Me." She only half learned them both and kept mixing them up, but I thought that was enough in one day for a little girl.

As I turned back to study, I gave her an empty evaporated milk can. The Mazatecs valued those cans, for sometimes they kept lard in them, or drank their coffee from them. Rosalia accidentally dropped the one I had given her and in doing so she discovered how nicely it rolled on the wooden floor. Ignoring us, she started rolling it back and forth, squealing with delight whenever it banged against a table leg. In between squeals she half sang and half talked. "Jesus loves me—saved you and your house!"

Concentration on language study became difficult at that moment, but if that was the topic of her chatter while she rolled a can on our floor, she would chant the same news while she bounced her baby sister at home. We wanted her family to hear it, so we let her shout and even helped her to get back on the tune once in awhile.

The hope that others would help to spread such news influenced many of our actions. It made us cordial to strangers, and to people from other villages. Perhaps it made me friendly to the man who stopped at our window to ask where Marta was. We did not know where she had gone, but we invited him in to wait for her. His name was José, and he was Marta's cousin from a village five hours away. He had brought her a gift of oranges.

While he waited, we helped him to read the leaflet of Bible verses. As he read he asked questions; he was not satisfied at merely reading correctly, he wanted to know the significance of its message as well. He had been concerned about life after death, and the paper told him that Jesus Christ was ready and waiting to clean up his heart and to make his admission into Heaven possible. To him the information was important; he took no chances on forgetting, but he read and reread the paper.

Still Marta had not come back, but if José delayed longer darkness would overtake him on the road. He decided to go, and we offered to pass his gift of oranges on to her. As he was leaving, we reminded him to tell his wife about the leaflet. "And my children," he added fervently.

José had interrupted our work by his visit, but it was one of those interruptions we were glad for. His visit gave a preview of how our work would be used, and as soon as he was gone, we turned back to it again. Florrie's fingers flew over the typewriter. ("Many nails jumping," said one little boy as he watched the keys hit the paper.) She was making four copies, for she wanted one for Inés. Inés now read fluently, and she enjoyed the Gospel so much that we hated to make her wait for a printed copy. In fact, Florrie could not even type the material fast enough to suit her. Sometimes she stood quietly at Florrie's shoulder reading the words as they appeared on the paper before her.

At last the typing was done, and we set about proofreading the sixty pages of manuscript. Aside from checking on the actual letters, we read through it several times for the tone marks, and because they had been added by pen and ink, we had to proofread each copy separately. We went through it to check verse, chapter, and page numbers. We read through it again to be sure that no words were left out between the bottom of one page and the top of the next. Another time, to be sure we had not omitted a verse or two at the end of some chapter— we had been warned about that type of mistake. If we stopped typing for some reason, it would have been natural to start again at the beginning of a chapter, forgetting that we had not finished the previous one.

But even then we were not done. The printer needed a statement of the Mazatec syllable. It had to be described clearly enough so that he could correctly divide any word that might otherwise go beyond the end of the line. We wrote up our rules and then leafed through the manuscript to make certain that they applied to every possible situation.

Now, what? Well, something for the cover. And the title page. And the reverse side of the title page. Then a sigh, "Well I guess. . . ." Yes. Finished!

That evening when the last neighbor was gone, and the door was shut for the night, we sat in our most comfortable chairs—folding ones with canvas seat and back—and took turns reading the translation aloud. The words were music to our ears, and we did not stop until we had read all twenty-one chapters.

As we took the manuscript to the post office the next day, we commented on how honored the Mexican government and Uncle Sam were, to be trusted with such a precious package. Mentally we followed its journey, the day it would be on donkey back, the day it would switch to a truck, then to a train. We estimated when it would arrive in New York. Then we wondered when we would have the completed book back, but we had nothing by which to calculate that date.

In the meantime life went on much as usual, except that Florrie took time to catch up on some things she had let slide those past few weeks. Our neighbors probably saw no change whatever, for the rest of the New Testament still lay ahead, and we continued to work at our desks and to teach our visitors.

José dropped in again. He had made it a habit of visiting us whenever he came to town, and each time he came we read some portion of John together. This time I put the story of the crucifixion on the table in front of him. Slowly he started to read chapter 18, while I stood beside him ready to help. Verse 3 told of Judas' arriving with the armed officers. In verse 6 José read: "As soon then as he had said unto them, I am he, they went backward, and fell to the ground."

Immediately José stopped reading, leaned back in his chair and chuckled softly. I looked over his shoulder and quickly reread the verse, looking for the error that had caused his amusement. I could not find it. The verse seemed all right to me, but he was still chuckling. I glanced over the preceding verses and saw no trouble, so I gave up and waited for his explanation. "They could not have done a thing to Him without His permission!" he said joyfully. I nodded in agreement, too awed to comment. His chuckle was not because of an error, instead it had been pure delight in the power of the Lord. That is what we had been working for. In a small way the manuscript was already serving its purpose.

CHAPTER XII

Reciprocity

(FALL OF 1942)

DURING THE SUMMER I taught again at the Summer Institute of Linguistics where many of the 130 students were preparing to go to Mexico. We of the staff were watching those students with special interest for we knew that our association with them would not end with the summer, rather a closer contact would begin.

When the courses were over, some of us traveled with them to Mexico City, serving them as interpreters and pointing out interesting things along the way. In Mexico City Florrie as group secretary helped them to change their dollars into pesos, and to put their passport papers in order. She continued in the office while another old-timer and I went to help two of the new workers to get started in another tribe. It took us about a month to make a trip through the tribe, decide in which village they should live, and help them to get settled and under way on the language work there.

Meanwhile George Cowan, one of the students that summer, arrived in Mexico. Florrie helped him with his papers, going with him to the embassy and to other government offices. When I got back to

Mexico City, one of my co-workers asked me, "Do
you not think George and Florrie would make a
nice-looking couple?" As Florrie and I were preparing to leave for Chalco, several of them slipped up
with a teasing, "Watch out, you will lose your partner."

That was possible, but I knew that she had committed her life to the Lord, and so had I. I did not
know just how my life would change when she married, but the Lord's promise that all things would
work together for good had been made to both of
us. If I remembered to trust Him, I could relax
while I waited to see what He would bring to pass.
So, with those thoughts in the back of my head, we
left as usual for the Mazatecs.

It rained most of the way over the trail, and by
the time we reached the foot of the Chalco mountain, we had been in the rain eleven hours. It had
been too muddy and slippery to rest by walking,
and so we tried to get relief by changing our posi-
tions in the saddle. Esteban, our guide, had given
up the struggle, and had stopped in a roadside sa-
loon for the comfort of drink. Marcos stayed with
us, but we missed Esteban. He had urged our animals on with a smack of his lips and a whack of
his whip, but Marcos had energy enough only to
keep the one pack animal moving. We had to
smack our own chapped lips and swing tired legs
against the mules' ribs.

The most traveled trail zigzagged up the mountain to the center of town, but Florrie and I did
not want to take it; we did not want to be seen so
drenched and dirty. We forgot that we would have

been a more startling sight if we had arrived clean after such a trail. Anyway, we turned up the short-cut that went directly to our house.

At first we traveled all right, but the trail became steeper, and the mules slipped on the hard-packed clay. Farther on they stopped and refused to move. If Florrie and I had ever wanted to ride it was then, but the mules were more stubborn than we were. When we got off to lead them, we ourselves could not stand on the slick path, and when we stepped into the cornfield beside it, we sank to our ankles in mud. We knew that home was just up the hill and around the corner, but the effort needed to get there seemed tremendous.

"Hello," called a friendly voice. We looked up and saw Inés and Catarina coming toward us from the top of the hill. For an hour they had watched us come down the mountain across the valley, and had waited another hour while we climbed the Chalco side. I tried to smile at them, but even my face muscles were tired, and my smile felt twisted. Inés took the rope of Florrie's mule and pulling, led him up the last stretch. Her bare feet did not slip on the clay as our shoes had done. "Come on!" she said to the mule. "You have been too long already."

Catarina, dignified as always, walked behind us. Just having them there rested us—maybe the mules felt the same way. Something made them walk faster, and before Catarina could tell us half the news, we were turning into our yard at home.

You would have thought that the trip over the trail would have been exercise enough to last us six months, but we studied better if we went out once in awhile. Not only that, but we liked to meet people from other parts of the tribe. So, Florrie and I took a walk every once in awhile.

One day when we went, Tomás and a friend of his got their kites and went with us. By the time we had reached the top of the mountain, five other boys had joined us. They all carried kites and every time the path neared the ridge they stopped and tried the breeze. Kite flying seemed to be more enjoyable with us to applaud, and when they found we were interested, they showed us the sticky bulbs which they used as paste in making the kites. They showed us the trees from which they made toy popguns, and the pulp they used as shot.

Each tree had a different name, and when I wrote them down it encouraged them to bring twigs from other trees, and to throw pebbles at those farther down the bank. Writing the new Mazatec words was no problem, the boys pronounced them clearly and I was used to the alphabet, but I did not know what they were called in English! I knew elderberry, and alder, and sycamore, but the other Mazatec names went into my dictionary with no English translation. I did try to describe them and the boys added any information they thought pertinent. This one made good firewood; the leaves from that one made medicine for stomach ache, etc.

Walking along we were just a group of friends sharing knowledge. Florrie's and my contribution was to tell them about the One who had made the trees and the rest of the world, and we sang hymns to teach them about Jesus who died to save them.

They must have been interested in our contribution because the next day two of them came and stood by our window. I could tell that they wanted something, but they were too bashful to say what it was. Tomás made himself their mouthpiece. He came to the window and called in, "They want to read." I took the leaflet of Bible verses and a pointer and went to the window.

"O.K. Let's read."

The bigger one pushed the smaller one, the smaller one pushed the bigger one, "She says for you to read." Neither one would permit himself to be pushed closer than about five feet from me. So I called to Tomás. "Tomás, you read first."

Without hesitation he came over and began, "Jesus said, I am the way . . ." By the time he was as far as, "Verily, verily, I say unto you . . ." the boys were at the window watching the pointer travel back and forth across the page.

"Now it is your turn," I said to them. Tomás silently went back to building a new kite, and as I pointed to the words, the older boy repeated them after me. He could not read, so I helped him to memorize. I was afraid that he might have been bored, but the next day he was back again. This time, however, he himself did not try to read, instead he pushed forward another boy. It was his brother Gil, and he had been to school. He had never read in Mazatec, but he picked it up so quickly that I let him read a Bible story as well as the leaflet.

When he had finished the story, I told him to take it home and read it to his family, and that if he would bring it back again, I would let him have a different one. That system worked well with a number of people. Because the stories were only typed, I could have let them keep only a few, but by lending them I could use the same story with different people. Some returned as many as eight times to exchange one story for another.

Gil became one of those who read regularly, but he never lost his shyness. Even though I put a chair behind him, he stood while he read. He never spoke voluntarily, and except for the words he used in reading, his vocabulary seemed to consist of "Mmm." The night he read the Christmas story, I told him that he did well, but he only said, "Mmm."

He did not leave as soon as he usually did, and I wondered if he wanted something. Then he put his hand into his pocket, pulled out three eggs, and handed them to me. When I thanked him for the gift, again his response was "Mmm."

A few days later a boy came and stood at our window. When I invited him inside, he said, "No," and continued to stand. After awhile I invited him in again. "No, I just came to look at you," he said.

When he did not want to come in, I decided to teach him through the window, and I started with, "Verily, verily, I say unto you, He that heareth . . ."

"Huh," said the boy, "I know that one. The paper you gave my brother has it." He was right, it was one of the verses in the leaflet.

Then he began to recite it and Florrie looked up from her desk. We had hoped that the Mazatecs would teach each other, because the News would spread much faster that way, but this was the first time we had heard a Mazatec recite a verse that we ourselves had not taught him. The boy's scorn thrilled us, for through it we learned that someone besides ourselves had been passing the Word along. We wondered who that someone was, and looking at the boy more closely, we recognized his resemblance to Gil.

The next day Gil was back for another story, and instead of leaving as soon as his lesson was finished, he continued to stand by the desk. At last he spoke. "If you have grace [that was the Mazatec way of saying *please*]." He started again, "My mother says would you have grace and copy these papers for us? We want them to keep."

I hesitated; I would have loved to copy the stories for him, but if I did when would I have time to translate new ones? If I let him keep the copy he already had, what would I do for the other people who were reading? I had been using the same copy over and over.

Gil saw my hesitation. "Have grace, my father says he will pay you." He was not begging, from under his shirt he pulled six sheets of typing paper. New and clean they had been bought for us. Undoubtedly they would give us money too, if we asked for it. Still I hesitated, and Gil spoke again. "My father says, if you are too busy, have grace, and give us the first stories back again. I will copy them." So I gave him the first stories back, and he went home to copy, probably with a stubby pencil, the Word of God that he and his family had come to recognize as precious.

CHAPTER XIII

At Bedtime

(SPRING OF 1943)

ONE EVENING while Florrie and I were eating supper, Inés pushed open the door, dropped her blanket on the floor and announced quietly, "I am sleeping here tonight."

We were startled, but if we had been Mazatecs we would have anticipated it. Inés' brother was away and since it was not the custom for a woman to sleep in a house alone, she had come to spend the night with her neighbors—us. Ours was the most logical place for her to come, for it was close enough so that she could hear a coyote after the chickens, or a thief breaking into her house. Catarina's house was close too, but Esteban, her husband, drank more and more frequently, and Inés wisely preferred our house to his.

We poured her a cup of tea and asked her to join us. She did and as soon as she had finished, she stood up, reached for a towel and said, "I'll help with the dishes." That was the polite thing to do; the Mazatecs helped with the work wherever they were staying.

Inés was completely at ease, confident that she would fit in. Florrie and I were not so sure. We did not know how much we should alter our habits for the benefit of our new roommate. We decided to make our bedtime more nearly approximate to her customary one, so when she folded up her sewing, we put aside our studying and helped her make a place to lie down.

In our one-room house most of the space was already occupied, but we pulled the table nearer the stove, and spread a mat for her between the table and the foot of our cots. To us it did not seem right to put a guest to bed on the floor, but it was what Inés expected. She told us good night, and then lay down, wrapping herself completely in a blanket that neither her head nor her feet were showing. The simplicity of her preparation for sleep made our nightly ritual seem so silly that we were glad her eyes were covered.

When morning came she got up early and slipped out quietly, but she left her blanket, a sign that she intended to be back again that night. She did come back, and for a number of nights after that. Her brother was making trips to other parts of the tribe buying donkeys and pigs. By driving them back and selling them at the Chalco price, he was able to make a small profit. Some trips took him three or four days, and while he was gone, Inés slept in our house.

One evening after we had become more accustomed to our roommate, we explained to her that we usually read the Bible and prayed before going to bed, and we suggested that the three of us do it together. Her eyes sparkled with interest as she waited to see our suggestion carried through.

Florrie and I quoted a verse in Mazatec, then Inés did too. After that we all bowed our heads and each of us prayed.

A few evenings later Catarina and Tomás came in, and since Florrie and I intended that our evening hours be spent studying, we gave them magazines to look at while we went on working. But they were not satisfied. After awhile Catarina spoke up, "We came to pray." Inés had told them about our prayer times and they had come to join us.

They were back again the following night, but they recognized it as bedtime before we did, and they began to prod us with their whispers, "Let's go home; I'm sleepy."

"Keep still," one of the others answered, "they are going to pray soon." When we heard that, Florrie and I laid down our pens and said, "Let's pray." They grinned and relaxed; they had stirred us to action at last.

Without being planned as such by us, the evenings became a time when the neighbors gathered to study about Christ. Even when Inés' brother was home she came over for a little while in the evening, and both she and Catarina brought any visitors they might have. The newcomers fitted right in, but their first prayers were very simple. Usually they said, "Father, help us to sleep well. Amen." After they gained confidence, one of them thanked the Lord that He heard and understood even though they were not "wise in words."

Florrie and I wanted them to know that the Lord was interested in them as individuals, so, when it was our turn, we prayed for Inés' brother and asked that he have a safe journey. Our neighbors reciprocated by praying for us, and one night Catarina said, "Bless the white-headed women as they study our language, for it is You who gives them the grace to help us."

They helped us too. Perhaps the most important thing they did was to answer our questions about the Mazatec language, and about the way they did things. Of course we were not the only ones asking questions. Usually they followed their answer with, "How do people do it in your country?" Often we spent more time answering questions than they did.

One evening they asked the question that they had been asking periodically for seven years, "When are you going to get married?"

Other years I had laughed at them, or had countered with, "Why do you want us to get married? If we marry we might leave this village and go to live in his." And I would quote one of their own proverbs, "It is the man who rules."

That night, however, I waited for Florrie to answer, but she did not speak up fast enough, and Catarina and Inés were quick to catch the hesitation. "You are getting married soon!" they shouted at her. Maybe I should have helped her out, but I was curious too, so I just waited. Then they changed to the question, "Are you going to get married?"

Florrie answered, "I do not know. I might some day. Why should I not?" Catarina and Inés fell silent. They were convinced that the day was not far off.

Florrie and I tried to spend a minimum of time

with small talk. The evening hours were for us some of the most important of the day. That was when we did our best desk work, but gradually we began spending more time with the people, singing hymns, and studying a portion of the Bible. We found ourselves planning for the evenings and wondering who the visitors would be.

Reina, Inés' aunt, was one of the most frequent visitors. She lived a considerable distance from Chalco, but when she shopped there, she stayed overnight with Inés. She listened carefully to the lesson, and requested that we sing, "Jesus Walks with Me." Then she explained that she liked that one because "He walked in with me from the farm." That was true. Florrie and I wanted them to know too, that the Lord could help them with their everyday problems.

The opportunity came when Inés was worried about her corn. The traditional planting season was almost at an end; her brother was away, and she had not been able to hire anyone to do the work. That night we prayed that she might find someone to plant her corn for her. Inés was embarrassed at having her private affairs brought before God, but the next day she was able to hire help, and after that their prayers were a bit more specific.

Catarina needed some very specific help. When Esteban was drunk, he banged around the house making everybody's life miserable. Then one night Catarina whispered urgently at our door, "Let me in."

Esteban was worse than usual, and she had slipped over to get out of his way. Softly so that he would not hear, she sobbed out her tale. He had hit her. She was not going back. In the morning she was leaving forever. We comforted her, lent her a blanket, and suggested she sleep on our floor. Esteban soon discovered that she was gone, and we could hear him calling and muttering outside.

When morning came, Catarina did not leave him. We were not surprised, for she had made similar threats before. She did wish that he would stop drinking, and so did we. We wished he had more schooling; if only he would read the Gospel and believe what he was reading, the Lord would take away his thirst for liquor.

We had tried to help him to read, but he had quit, embarrassed because Tomás did better than he did. We decided to try again, so a few days later I called him into the house. As I pulled up a chair beside him, I was wondering what I should do. I could not imagine him praying, and yet I knew that his wife had told him about our prayer times, and he knew that others prayed before they read. If we started to read without prayer, his feelings might be hurt because I was not treating him the same as I did his family. I decided that this time I would not ask him, but I would pray myself instead.

I bowed my head, but before I got my mouth open, he had begun. He said, "God, whose is the world, thank You for saving me. God, whose is the world, help me to read this paper. That is all I am going to say." I was thrilled that he had prayed, but later I decided that he had done it from mimicry and not conviction. After a few lessons, he found excuses for not reading, and drank as much as ever.

Even if Esteban was disappointing in his actions, Inés was pure delight. She had not only learned to read Mazatec, but she was writing it too. Tomás came in one day, his eyes sparkling with fun, and told us that he was the mailman. He gave us a letter from Inés which said, "Hello, how are you? Please come visit me. I have a little party. We give each other gifts because God gave us a gift. He sent His Son to the world."

Just before we left the house she sent a second note asking for the loan of the "irons that you eat with." So when we went we took our silverware with us. The silverware was just one of our foreign customs that she had prepared for. On one side of each place was a "mouth cloth," and on the other was a glass of water. "You can drink that," she told us the minute we entered, "I cooked it." Then she served us a delicious dinner—chicken, rice, *tortillas,* coffee flavored with cinnamon.

Chatting with her while we ate, I happened to see beyond her to a shelf over on the wall. It was empty! For years it had held a picture and a perpetually burning candle—and probably the picture was contrary to the Lord's command, "Thou shalt have no other gods before me." Without even telling us about it, Inés had quietly disposed of both the candle and the picture. Florrie noticed the empty shelf too, and we were both delighted enough to do most anything Inés wanted.

For days she had been urging us to make a trip to Reina's farm, and we decided that we would take a day off and go. The farm was a two-and-a-half-hours' walk from Chalco, but Inés put up bean sandwiches and sweetened coffee for a lunch at the halfway point.

We started at nine in the morning, but soon my arms were burning in the hot sun. Inés scolded me for not wearing long sleeves and I defended myself by saying that I wanted to do things the way they did them. Her answer was one of disgust. "Our skins are dark and tough, and the sun does not hurt us. Your skin is white and tender. We know the sun hurts you, and we would understand why you were wearing sleeves." She was right; it was foolish to try to be like them in all things.

As we topped the mountain closest to Reina's house, her children saw us. They dashed through the cornfields and joined us, escorting us to the hut. Reina welcomed us in, and her friends from the surrounding huts came to greet us. Living so far from Chalco, most of them had never met us before and they marveled that we were able to talk with them. Children filled the doorway, but they gave way and let a white-haired woman come in. As she entered, Reina placed a chair for her, and the others stopped talking, conceding to her the right to direct the conversation.

She pulled her chair closer, and looking up into our faces, asked, "What is it you do before going to bed?" At first I did not understand, but then I realized that news of our evening meetings must have reached them. Florrie was already answering, and not only the old lady, but the others were listening too.

"Sing for us," one of them asked later. So we sang "Christ the Lord Is Risen Today" and "Only Believe." They asked for more and more hymns until Reina put food on the table and told them to let us eat. As they left, several of them said, "Thank you for telling us about God."

They would not have understood if I had tried to thank them for the pleasure they had given me. In them I had seen a group of people eager to hear about the Lord. In fact, they had already heard from Inés and Reina, and if they did not believe in Him, they seemed ready to do so.

We were thoughtful as well as happy when we returned from Reina's farm. The visit had helped me to see beyond Chalco to hundreds of villages the size of Reina's and larger. Florrie and I could never reach them all. We needed help from somewhere— from George Cowan perhaps. If he and Florrie worked in Chalco, I could get another partner and work in some other village.

CHAPTER XIV

A New Partner

(FALL OF 1944)

THE MAZATEC TRIBE gained when Florrie and George were married, because George put his shoulder to the wheel and helped with the translation work. But I was not so sure about myself. Florrie's and my partnership had been a good one and I wondered who would take her place.

I did not need anyone immediately, because when the Cowans went back to the tribe, I took a furlough. Then I taught the usual three months at the Summer Institute of Linguistics. Teaching linguistics was getting to be a habit with me, but it was the subject, not the geographical location that remained the same. In the summer of 1944 I was sent to Canada to teach in the branch school that was just opening there. I enjoyed it very much, but even so, I was glad when the time came to head back to Mazatec land.

Out in Chalco the Mazatecs gathered around and stared at Helen Black, the new member of Wycliffe Bible Translators, who had gone back with me. They watched her admiring the mountain view and one said to another, "She's glad she came." So few outsiders were really glad to be in their town that her enthusiasm was one of the first things they noticed.

They saw her amusement as she peeled sixteen marble-size potatoes for our dinner (two of us) and they said, "She likes to laugh."

They tested her on a few phrases in Mazatec and when she could answer their greetings they told me very solemnly, "Her head is soft." They were right, she was intelligent, but she was also working hard. She was copying and memorizing words from the dictionary file; she was memorizing parts of the Bible stories, and perhaps more important, as soon as she had memorized something, she was using what she knew in conversation. Of course she frequently made mistakes, but when she did she chuckled, apparently getting as much fun from those mistakes as the Mazatecs did.

When I was beginning, I had not recognized many of my own mistakes, but by watching Helen I could see the type of thing I must have done hundreds of times. There was the day we went to market. On our way home a little girl caught up to us. She was carrying a pop bottle, dangling it from her finger by a string. That was a common sight. People used kerosene to start their fires in the morning and that was the way they carried it.

Just to be friendly, Helen asked, "Where have you been?"

The little girl answered, "I went to buy some whisky." The pop bottle had fooled us that time.

Helen recognized the word for "I went to buy" and jumped to the conclusion that the rest of the

44403

sentence was the word for "kerosene," so she answered, "That's good."

Many times when Helen made an obvious mistake, our friends would say encouragingly, ". . . she'll learn." I was not quite sure of the meaning of the first syllable of that sentence. I wrote it down, thought of the different ways I had heard it used, and came to the conclusion that they were saying, "Soon she will learn."

Then one day I was telling Catarina about the law in parts of the United States. I said that when a man went to jail for murder, he stayed much longer than a Mazatec murderer did. I said that he would stay at least twenty years. Catarina was very much impressed and she asked with awe, ". . . . will he get out?" There was that same syllable. But this time it could not mean "soon," because I had already told Catarina that a man stayed in at least twenty years. I thought again of the sentences in which I had heard that syllable. Then I had it. It did not mean "soon," it meant "eventually." Our friends had been saying of Helen, "Eventually she'll learn."

One of the first things she learned was to sing the Mazatec hymns, and she taught them to the children who came to the house. Two little girls who came frequently were seven-year-old Blanca, and six-year-old Tecla. They loved to sing and learned several hymns, but "Jesus Loves Me" was their favorite. Helen wanted to give them a choice in the songs, so she asked Blanca, "Now which?" Very bashfully she answered, "Jesus." So they sang "Jesus Loves Me" again.

After singing another song, Helen turned to Tecla and asked, "Now which?" Tecla with extreme shyness pulled her shawl across her face until only her eyes showed above it, but finally she managed to say, "Jesus." Then her shawl dropped and she forgot her bashfulness when they began to sing again.

Our hopes that their family shared their enthusiasm for Jesus received a jolt a little later. An older sister came to the house to borrow a handkerchief. I knew that they did not need the handkerchief for ordinary use, and I suspected that the request had something to do with witchcraft. The girl saw my hesitation and urged me with, "I will bring it right back."

"Why do you want it?" I asked her gently. Then it was her turn to hesitate; she did not want to tell me, but she knew of no other way to get the handkerchief. She told me that her baby brother was sick, that the witch doctor said that he had been frightened by us, and that he would get well only if they waved one of our handkerchiefs in front of his face. The diagnosis had been based on the fact that we had passed their house a day or two before the baby became ill.

"You know better than that," I told her. "Do you not remember that when Blanca was little we fixed the sores on her legs, and when Tecla was little we fixed a cut on her face?" The girl did remember and she was embarrassed as she said, "I do not know why he was frightened, none of the others have been." But she still thought that what the man had said was true.

I wondered whether or not I should send the handkerchief. If I refused and the baby died, they would consider it my fault. If I sent it and the baby got better, it would be proof to them that the witch doctor was right. The big sister knew that I did not believe the witch doctor, but in the end I let her take a handkerchief. As soon as she had it, she left for home on the run. It did not take long, she soon was back smiling and grateful.

Her family had been a disappointment, but our nearer neighbors had been doing better. They had been gathering together and growing as they studied some mimeographed Bible lessons that the Cowans had made while I was on furlough.

For the first Bible study after our return, we used one of those lessons. Each person present had a copy, and they took turns reading aloud a sentence at a time. Catarina was a poor reader, and she had to be helped over most of the words—it was a triumph of prayer and patience that she read at all. Inés was a fluent reader, and the others watched the words eagerly, almost hoping for a chance to correct her. Ramón, Marta's brother, tried to give the impression of fluency, but the eyes of the others were too sharp, again and again they corrected him.

Then it was Helen's turn. Deep silence. Everybody was waiting to see what she would do with the paper. They knew that she had been there only a short time, and that she spoke only the simplest sentences. She drew a long breath and began. Slowly, carefully, she read in good understandable Mazatec. She read so slowly that it seemed an age before she finished the sentence, but when she did, Catarina burst out with, "How can she read when she cannot talk?"

"It is because she knows how each letter is supposed to sound," I answered. They accepted the explanation, but they were still amazed. And it made even me appreciate the linguistic courses.

Having studied linguistics, Helen could use the Cowans' and my materials while she was waiting for her memory to catch up with her tongue. From her point of view, to read Mazatec was merely a matter of pronouncing the sounds that were being signaled by the sequence of letters. She could do this even though she had no idea what the various words meant.

That was possible because Florrie and I had figured out how many different signaling sounds the Mazatecs used in speech, and to each one of those sounds we had assigned a different letter. We had chosen to represent the sounds with letters that corresponded with the Spanish alphabet. That seemed best because Ramón, Gil, or any other Mazatec who had been educated in Spanish, could read a Mazatec story with a minimum of help from us. And Tomás who had learned to read in Mazatec could read Spanish too.

We were always trying to find ways to help the people to read. A good primer would be one of the best answers, but the first two editions of our primers had been too hard. I had introduced my words too fast, and by the time they reached the tenth lesson the students had slowed almost to a halt. It took a lot of persistence to get over the next lessons and some of the students made it, and some did not. I made another primer, and in that one I put more review, and cut the hard lessons in half.

But even a good primer would not be enough. If they were to read the Gospel of John and after that the New Testament, the people needed to practice on something more difficult than a primer, but not as hard as Scripture. I decided to translate a book about the Mexican national heroes, and I hoped it would be easy enough for the people to enjoy after they had finished the primer.

I used a schoolbook for a model, but I did not follow it exactly, partly because of the dates. Many of the Mazatec-speaking folks did not even know the date of the current year, so the fact that Benito Juárez was born in 1806 did not mean a thing to them. In my story I said, "Juárez was born about a hundred and forty years ago." That really impressed them. They who knew almost no history about their own tribe were amazed that a man who was still as well known as Juárez should have been born that long ago.

In the story about Bolívar, the hero of South America, the only word I had for "liberator" was the one I was using in reference to Christ for "saviour." I tried to find a word that would make a distinction, but finally decided that at least in Mazatec the words were the same.

After I had those two stories done, I helped Catarina to read them. She liked them so well that she borrowed them for Esteban. When he sent them back a few days later, he sent an old history book along with them and asked that I translate that one too.

That fall in addition to the work on the hero stories, I arranged words for several hymn tunes. We had found that one of the quickest ways to the people's hearts was through singing. Frequently people memorized the hymns and sang them to their friends and relatives at home. For that reason when there was some truth that we wanted them to remember, we found a hymn with that message and translated it.

Then one day a woman I did not know came to call. Her question after the usual greeting was, "Do you have medicine for fear?" Two years before, her house had been struck by lightning and had burned down. Since that time she had not been well, and her friends told her that fear was making her sick. I questioned her in the hopes of making a different diagnosis, but was not successful, so I acted on the assumption that her friends were correct.

The best medicine I knew for either deep-seated fear, or for temporary jitters was an assurance that a powerful God loves us and is in control of all things. We talked to her about Him and helped her to memorize a Bible verse. But I was not satisfied. It seemed to me that we should have a hymn that such people could sing when afraid. That night, with her in mind, I put words to the tune "God Will Take Care of You."

The next day Helen and I took a walk to the woman's section of town. We did not know her name, but we found her by inquiring for the woman ill with fear sickness. We taught her the new hymn and she and her family were very appreciative.

Our neighbors liked that song too, but when we met for Bible study they were not satisfied to sing just one or two hymns. Every night the request was, "Let's sing all of them." At that time we had twenty-five hymns, but that is what we did, we sang them all.

Sometimes Tomás was the song leader who gave the pitch and set the speed. The next night it was Inés. But those two good friends did not work together very well. When Tomás was leading, Inés raced ahead. When Inés was leading, Tomás teased her by interrupting and telling her that she had started too low. It made me remember the tales I had heard of troubles in a church choir, but I had not expected it to happen in a congregation of seven.

They understood portions of Scripture more easily than they had done. Typical were their comments on the Bible lesson from John 2:13-22. The verses told how Christ had cleaned out the temple in Jerusalem, objecting to the things He had found in His Father's house.

Since, when we believe in Christ, we too are temples of God, we applied that to ourselves. We discussed the things that needed to be cleaned out of our hearts. Tomás mentioned thievery, Ramón lust, Inés lying. When we discussed things that should come into our hearts, Catarina suggested love, and Ramón life and truth.

One night after everybody had read one of a series of verses, I asked each person, "Which one

did you like, and why?" When Tomás put his
finger on Psalm 51:5, I asked, "Is that the one you
like?"

He answered, "I don't like it, but it says that I
was born in sin."

I went on calling on the others, and I did it as
they would have done. Before each girl's name I
put the title "Miss" (it meant both "Miss" and
"Mrs.," and was even used with animals). In front
of the boys' names I put the title "Mister" (it was
used for people, animals, and even birds). I called
on "Miss Catarina," and then on "Miss Inés." After
that it was Ramón's turn. But when I called on
him I said, "Miss Ramón." Everybody but Ramón
shouted with glee.

That mistake had been just a slip of the tongue,
but I made other errors through ignorance, and I
just had to hope that none of them would be seri-
ous. There was the night that I asked Reina's son
to pray. He had not been to the Bible studies very
much, so he hesitated about leading in prayer. To
help him out I prayed sentence by sentence and let
him repeat it after me. Right in the middle of a
sentence I heard myself make a mistake in Mazatec.
"What will he do now?" I thought. Would he copy
my error? Would he come to a complete halt rather
than repeat such a barbarous thing? Would he rise
above it? I waited, trying to think what I would
do if it stopped him. Of course it seemed an age,
but actually it was only a few seconds before he
reached the spot. He hesitated at my "you is," corrected it to "you are," and went on. His prayer
reached Heaven grammar perfect, and I breathed a

sigh of relief. It would have been a shame if he had been embarrassed during his very first public prayer.

Of course his prayer was not very public. That is, only old friends of his were there. Helen and I would have liked to have had others come, but for some reason almost no one had.

Some evenings later a young man, a stranger, did come to the Bible study. Helen and I were delighted, and we immediately made him welcome by passing him a hymnbook, and helping him to read a bit. Then Catarina came in. With no preliminaries her tongue lashed out. He was a spy! He had just come to see what we were doing!

I broke in to stop the tirade, but even in her surrender she grieved us. She finished off with, "Do you not go around telling people what we say?" But that was just what we wanted him to do. We were thrilled when those we had been teaching taught others. Christ said: "Go ye into all the world and preach the gospel to every creature." That did not apply just to Helen, the Cowans, and me; it applied to our neighbors too. Would Catarina, in fear of ridicule, wall off the Gospel and keep the knowledge of eternal life shut up to herself and her handful of friends?

CHAPTER XV

Checking In

(SPRING OF 1945)

LATE ONE AFTERNOON Margarita, the wife of one of the town butchers, came to the door. She was in such a hurry that she hardly even greeted us. She asked us to go with her to help a woman who had been gored by a bull. I got out my basket with medicines and emergency supplies, and as we hurried along, she told us how it had happened.

In order to get meat for market, her husband bought cattle from people in distant villages, then drove the cattle back and slaughtered them in Chalco. The preceding day they had brought back a bull, and that afternoon their ten-year-old son led it home from pasture. Everything was fine until a dog barked and frightened the bull. He pulled away from the boy and ran down the path with the dog at his heels.

An old partially-blind lady heard the running animal, but thinking it was a donkey she just stepped to the side of the path. The bull lowered his head and gored her in the thigh.

Chalco law makes the owner responsible for anyone hurt by an animal, so the old lady walked a mile to the center of town and told Margarita and

her husband she was going to complain to the town
authorities. They said, "Complain if you want to,
but get fixed up first." So the old lady went home,
and Margarita came up to get us.

She did not know where the injured woman lived,
nor even her name, but she inquired her way along
with, "Where is the woman who was hurt?"

Chalco's most thickly populated district stretched
about a mile along the side of the mountain, but
finally we were in the right section. A neighbor of
the injured woman led us to a poor tumble-down
shack. She called, "Are you there?" No answer.
Margarita called, "Are you there?" No answer. The
neighbor and Margarita looked at each other, and
then slowly pushed the door open.

There on the dirt floor, on a straw mat, lay the
woman. Her skirt was torn and covered with blood.
Margarita said, "Hello. We have brought you one
wise in the way of medicine. She speaks our language. She will fix you well."

The woman grunted in response, and to those of
us standing over her, nothing could have sounded
more beautiful. After a bit of coaxing she rolled
over and let me look at her. Oh! A great big gaping
wound. I suppose the bull had intended to get
her in the trunk, but the Mazatec costume with its
long full tunic had fooled him and his horn had
entered her upper thigh. If it had been four inches
higher that would have been the end of the little
old lady.

I knelt on one side of her and Helen on the
other, and we started to pull the wound together.
The old lady began to object but Margarita shouted

at her, "Let her medicine you! Am I not the one who will have to pay if you die? Am I not the one who will have to bury you?" Margarita was referring to the Chalco law that the owner of a killing animal has to pay funeral expenses. The logic of her argument impressed the old lady and she let us fix her up.

In order to give her some aspirin, I went to the corner that was the kitchen for a cup and a bit of water. I found a cup, just one. There was also one bowl and one plate. It was the poorest home I had ever been in.

We went to see her every day for awhile, and usually Margarita took her a little food. She would not stay quiet, but the wound healed anyway and probably her general health was better because she moved around. The town officials kept their eye on the case, and since Margarita and her husband were taking care of the woman, they took no action. If they had not, then the town officials would have "gotten mad." I did not know just what that meant, but nobody wanted it to happen, and we were all relieved that the old lady made good progress.

By that time the Cowans had arrived from Mexico City, and they brought the most interesting thing possible from the Mazatecs' point of view—a brand-new baby boy. Everybody watched him with delight. One minute they were calling him a "saint" —queer that most church figures were blond—and the next minute they were laughing at his bald head. Most of their babies were born with black hair half an inch long, but Baby Paul's head was smooth and blond. They looked at him lovingly and, implying that he reminded them of their smooth round gourds, called him "Dipper head."

The Cowans rented a bedroom house from Marta, but they were eating with Helen and me. Every day Tomás took two pails and went to the village well. Sometimes he had to stand in line an hour and a half before he could fill them. Sometimes two hours. He would go twice a day and that meant that our household of four adults and a baby got along on four pails of water a day. With care everything ran smoothly despite the water shortage. It did take thought, however. We never took really clean water to wash our hands; instead we used the water in which we had washed vegetables, or the water in which eggs had boiled. The cooperation of the whole family was needed before one of us could have a shampoo.

Then one day Tomás managed to get us six pails instead of the usual four. Wonderful! I could wash my hair at last. "Save your rinse water for me," Florrie called. I did. She heated it up again and washed Paul's baby clothes in it.

The Cowans had delayed in Mexico City while they waited for Paul to become accustomed to this world. Now they were delighted to be back in Chalco, and they wanted to stay awhile. So when word came that Dr. Eugene A. Nida of the American Bible Society was in Mexico City, it was decided that Helen and I should be the ones to consult with him for all of us.

The Book of Acts was the thing in question. Florrie had translated most of it before she was married, and she had gone through it once more since then. Now she was ready for criticisms and suggestions from someone who knew translation problems and languages in general but not specifically Mazatec.

Helen and I decided to take a Mazatec-speaking person with us, just in case we wanted to check some of Dr. Nida's suggestions while we were still with him.

Prisca, a twenty-year-old girl, agreed to go with us. She had never been away from home, and her mother somewhat nervously put her in our care. "Remember, if she gets sick, you are to medicine her quickly." She gave instructions that way because when someone died in Chalco, people were apt to say, "He waited too long before he medicined himself."

Soon after arriving in Mexico City, Prisca got a toothache. She had had trouble with it off and on for five months, but because she had it again while she was with us that made it our responsibility. The only dentist we knew was one who treated the American colony, so we made an appointment with him. We knew he was expensive, but we did not want to take any chances with Prisca or her tooth.

His office was on the sixth floor, and Prisca's eyes opened wide as we went into the stone building and were whisked up in the elevator. We waited a little while and then it was our turn. The nurse told Prisca in rapid Spanish to rinse out her mouth. Prisca understood Spanish, but not that rapid-fire Mexico City kind, so she did not move until I translated the request into Mazatec. Then she picked up the glass and did it. The nurse spread the news that there was an Indian in the chair who understood no Spanish. The nurse from next door found business in our office and stayed long enough to look Prisca up and down very carefully. The doctor came in frankly curious, and his curiosity increased even more when I told him that Prisca had seen her first car less than a week before. He took a long squint at her teeth before settling down to the job at hand.

When he decided that the aching tooth needed to be pulled, I stood beside the chair ready to help.

"Tell her to spit," said the dentist in English.

"Spit," said I in Mazatec.

It was soon over and we were on our way out—the whole office staring after us. I gave Prisca a Kleenex and told her that people who lived in that kind of a house did not like it if someone spit on the floor.

"Mmm," said Prisca. She kept her mouth shut and her head high, and we made it to the street in safety.

Once the tooth had been taken care of, we settled down to the task of checking Acts. Dr. Nida sat with the Greek and the Spanish New Testament in front of him, and I with the Mazatec. My job was to look at the Mazatec and give him a quick literal translation into English. He compared what I said with the Greek, asked questions, and agreed or disagreed.

Among other things he pointed out that we had translated a number of Greek metaphors rather than the specific words. One example was found in Acts 14:8. "Being a cripple from his mother's womb" was the Greek expression, but no Mazatec ever says that. "Ever since he was born," Dr. Nida suggested. He emphasized the fact that it was the message we were supposed to get across, not just words.

We were busy reading the Mazatec and Spanish translations eight hours a day, and long before the eighth hour arrived, I was exhausted. After several days of it, I looked forward to Sunday, a day of rest—from reading the Bible! I had not supposed that reading the Bible would ever be a "labor" from which we would rest on Sunday, but that was what it was that week.

The days with Dr. Nida had been time well spent. Helen and I went back to the Cowans with a notebook full of suggestions and ideas that would provide dinner conversation for a month.

One bit under discussion was the Gospel of John. When we sent it to the American Bible Society in the spring of 1942, we had expected the completed book back soon. But time passed and we found out that the delay was due to the war. Because it was wartime, the printer had trouble getting the type necessary for some of the letters peculiar to Mazatec. Then at last the type was at hand. The printer got busy, and in 1945 we received and proofread the galleys. We were all excited. Soon the Mazatecs would have the Gospel of John! But—

There was something else to consider. The Gospel of John had been written with an alphabet which corresponded to Spanish. Now we were being urged to change to an alphabet that corresponded more closely to that used in a scientific publication.

If we were going to change, it seemed obvious that we should do so before the copies of the Gospel of John were made. We hated to do it. The Mazatecs needed those books. But we had learned a lot of Mazatec those last three years. If we made a complete revision of the Gospel of John, it would be a better job than the 1942 version had been. We could even apply the suggestions Dr. Nida had made for the Book of Acts. Well— (sigh) —O.K. We would change. (It was a mistake. In 1956 we changed back again.)

CHAPTER XVI

A New Village

(SPRING OF 1945)

HELEN AND I were planning to move. The Cowans were staying on in Chalco, and it seemed that more people could be told about the Lord if we were not all in the same place. The question was, to which village should we go? If it was one where the people spoke the same dialect as those in Chalco, we could continue helping with the New Testament translation. That was the one basic requirement, but we would take other things into consideration too.

First, water supply. Although there is considerable rain in the Mazatec area, there was frequently a shortage of water. Perhaps this was because the clay soil caused the rain to drain off instead of soaking in. Perhaps it was due to the big caves or sinkholes that were in the bottom of every valley. Whatever the reason, water in the dry season was scarce in Chalco. We hoped that we could move where there was a good water supply.

Second, a market. In many Mazatec towns the people met once a week to buy and sell. Chalco itself had a big market, and once a week we could buy meat, eggs, fruit, onions, tomatoes; and, in sea-

son, cabbage, squash, peas. A market was a big
convenience.

Third, altitude. The higher the altitude the
colder it was. Chalco was cold, but the cold was
helpful in that there were less insects there than at
lower altitudes, and the malarial mosquito was missing.

We started asking questions about the various
towns, and as usual when we wanted information,
our neighbors were our chief informants. In this
case, however, they were unwilling informants.
They did not want us to go; they liked to have
us around. But there was another reason for their
displeasure. To them, as to many Mazatecs, any
village not their own was "ugly."

We refused to take "ugly" as a complete description, and insisted on answers to specific questions.
Catarina always answered with great contempt in
her voice. The town where José lived, and into
which Amalia had married, was "windy," "foggy,"
"cold," and in hot weather there was "no water."

Marta's method was to tease, giving us information with such a twinkle in her eye that we wondered if she were telling the truth. According to
her one of the towns we mentioned had "no water."
It was low in altitude and therefore "hot." It had
"big spiders," "mosquitoes," and "scorpions." Then
she added, "You do not like bugs, do you, Eunice."

But even Marta dropped her teasing ways when
we mentioned Río Sancho. She agreed with Inés
who said, "We will not allow you to go there."
Catarina described the people as a "bunch of murderers." Well, murderers need to know about Christ

just as much as anybody else. And we were not sure that our neighbors knew what they were talking about, they were apt to think people of towns other than their own as "murderers." So we did not reject Río Sancho because of their description of it, but we did listen when they suggested the town of Río Seco as a compromise.

Río Seco was the place were Marta's sister had gone after her marriage. Everybody said there was a lot of fruit, plenty of water, and no malaria. Then Marta volunteered, "But there is no post office, how would you get your mail?" It was an eight-hour walk from Chalco, but in spite of Marta's thrust about "no mail," Helen and I immediately started making plans for a trip over. We wanted to see for ourselves what the place was like.

We set out to rent horses and to find someone who would guide us over. The first person we asked was willing to let us use his horses until he heard where we were going. Then his answer was a positive and final "no." His reason was that the trail was steep and rocky, and he was afraid that his horses would fall. Then he advised us not to go. "It is ugly," he told us.

We tried another place, and again the answer was "no." This man explained that the rocks were small and would hurt the horses' hoofs. Other times when we had wanted animals, somebody had been ready to let his animals go for a price, but no one would even discuss a price to this town.

There was no definite date by which we had to be over in Río Seco, so we did not let the refusals bother us. Somebody would rent us animals, and in the meantime the horse hunt gave us a good excuse for visiting around town. By the time people had talked to us about going, we were good friends and they were ready to listen to other things.

One woman was especially interested in Heaven. She had asked question after question; then as we stood up to leave she asked if we would buy some eggs. We said we would, but she did not get them for us. She said that her daughter would take them to us when she came from school. As we went out the door she leaned forward and whispered, "When my daughter goes up to your house, tell her about the One who is up in Heaven." We did, amused at the mother's clever management, and pleased that she wanted her daughter to hear.

When the daughter came, we not only told her about Heaven, but Helen taught her to sing too. Helen had made good progress in learning Mazatec. She got along well with the more common things like buying eggs and teaching the children hymns. Now she wondered if she might tell a Bible story some evening. She got out her flannelgraph materials and began to study the story of Daniel in the Lions' Den.

Many of the words in the story were new, but memorizing them was not the hardest part for her. The hardest part was overcoming a habit many of us English-speaking people have. When most English-speaking people stop to think, or when they are speaking in public, they say "ah" every few words. Well, "ah" is the sign of a question in Mazatec. If you say "ah-banana," that means, "Is it a banana?" If you say, "The boy went ah-school." That means,

"Was it school the boy went to?" If you say, "The boy ah-went school."? That means, "Did the boy go to school?"

Well, Helen had the "ah" habit, and instead of making statements, she was asking questions all the way through her story. Part of her trouble was because Mazatec was difficult for her, and she was thinking hard. But she did not use that "ah" as an excuse for not trying. She practiced, and practiced, and practiced some more. And she made it! The appointed evening came, she told her story, illustrating it with the flannel-backed figures and not an "ah" intruded. The neighbors were impressed. "Now she knows our language," was their comment.

It was just a few days later that a woman called and asked us to go down and give some vitamin shots to her daughter. The daughter, Celia, was married to a man who lived in Río Sancho. She had been ill for some time and her husband Rafael had brought her to Chalco to be with her mother. Then he had gone on to Tepetlán, told the doctor there about her, and had brought back some medicine. That was the medicine with which we injected her every other day.

One day as I was putting away my needle and syringe I told them that Helen and I wanted to move to another village, but that we did not know where to go. "Río Sancho!" the three shouted.

"Yes," I said, "we were thinking of Río Sancho, but everyone we ask says that the people there are bad people. They say they kill each other."

"That's not true." The mother started talking fast. But Rafael and Celia were silent, just looking at each other. Then Rafael said, "Yes, it is true that people have been killed over there, but nobody would kill you, you are not in politics." Politics. I had never been able to figure out what that word meant, it seemed to include everything from the business of a mayor to the ownership of property. Maybe he was right, anyway Helen and I knew nothing about running the town, and we owned no property.

They saw us hesitate and were quick to push their advantages. "We will send horses for you whenever you would like to go." We did not immediately set a date, so Rafael added, "Do you have household goods? We will send pack animals."

"Do you suppose someone would rent us a house?" I asked.

"My brother will," he answered immediately. Their eagerness almost took my breath away. We had been trying for weeks to get animals for a trip to Río Seco but without success. And now we had been offered riding animals, pack animals, and a house for Río Sancho! We wanted to go right then, but it was time for us to teach again at the Summer Institute of Linguistics. They begged us not to forget, and we promised that we would not. And so we parted, all of us hopeful, wondering what would happen in the fall.

CHAPTER XVII

Fruitful Labor

(FALL OF 1945—SPRING OF 1946)

THAT FALL I WAS DELAYED two months working on the grammar of Mazatec with my brother Ken. Much of the grammar Florrie and I had worked out some time previously, but a sizable chunk had hidden behind that elusive thing "tone." We had written the obvious differences of tone that distinguished such words as "horse" and "seed," but we had missed certain glides that in many verbs distinguished the first person from the third, and the second person singular from one of the plural persons.

That fall Ken and I lined up the verbs in a way that showed the regularities both of the tone and of the verbs' meaningful parts. By the time we had finished, not only was the material ready for technical publication, but I had a better idea of how the language worked as a whole.

While I had been taking advantage of Ken's help, Helen and Marion Doble had gone out to the tribe. Rafael and Celia heard that Helen was back, and they renewed their offer of riding animals and a house in Río Sancho. So while I was struggling with the tone of verbs, George Cowan helped Helen and Marion to settle in Río Sancho.

The house into which they moved was forty-six feet long, so he put in a partition and made them a private bedroom at one end of it. That was a luxury we had not had in Chalco. He also put up some bookshelves and did other things that men seem to do so easily and women with such effort. Then he went back to Chalco, and Helen and Marion stayed on with their new friends, the people of Río Sancho.

About a month later I arrived in Chalco. I stayed there three days visiting Florrie and George; then Ricardo, a servant of the girls' landlord, came to escort me to Río Sancho. He showed pride in his task almost every time we overtook people on the road. They would speed up to the pace of the mule, walk with us awhile and then ask my guide, "Where is she going?"

"To Río Sancho."

"Whose house will she be in?"

"Ours!" he would answer, claiming me through his boss.

Once as we traveled a man looked at me with an uncomplimentary expression on his face. Ricardo watched him, and as the man opened his mouth to speak, he warned, "Watch out! She understands us." That so amazed the man that he forgot to be rude. Time and again we saw our knowledge of the language both win us friends and hold off potential enemies.

In Río Sancho the people were delighted that Helen could talk with them, and they were pleased that Marion was trying, so they were all ready to welcome me too. There were friendly smiles everywhere as I rode into the village.

It was a very different type of town from Chalco. There we had lived on the side of a mountain and looked across the valleys to a green mountain range, and beyond to a darker green one, then a purple one, then another, and another, until the last was a faint outline against the sky. Río Sancho was in a narrow valley with mountains so steep and close that we had to tip our heads back to see the sky. The straight-ahead view on three sides showed coffee trees growing up between jagged rocks.

It was the coffee trees that shaped the lives of the people of Río Sancho, and those who owned the land on which it grew were "rích" in comparison with the others. There was no doubt that ownership of land brought in money, but it also made enemies of those coveting its coffee trees.

The first few days in town I was enchanted with the brook not far from our door. I loved the wrens that sang and scolded from our ridge pole, and the swish of the women's skirts as they passed on the road outside. It all sounded so peaceful! But that peacefulness was deceptive; it could be shattered by the exuberant shriek of a drunken man or by a whisper. The whispers were the worst.

There were whispers about our landlord Lino. They spoke of a quarrel with his oldest brother. There had been a fight, and some said that Lino had tried to kill his brother, some said that the brother had tried to kill Lino, but whichever they said, they said it softly and with a glance over their shoulders.

I glanced too. I saw Lino's tenderness with his daughter and felt that he must have been in the right. And yet? Everyone jumped to obey his spoken or gestured command. He never shouted. But he was boss. And he was boss of a lot of people. Besides his family there were at least four full-time hired men, a maid in the kitchen, and about thirty coffee pickers. Children picked coffee too, and some whole families worked for him.

The door of our house and that of our landlord's family opened onto the same yard and I watched the coffee pickers when they returned in the afternoon. Each one bent forward as he walked balancing a bag of coffee berries on his back. Then when he reached the cluster of people around Adela, Lino's wife, he lowered it, sighed, and sat on it, resting and chatting while he waited for Adela's attention.

Adela was the bookkeeper and cashier. From a distance she seemed completely relaxed as she leaned smiling against a rock. All eyes were on Ricardo, the hired man, as he picked up a sack and poured the coffee into a five-gallon kerosene can. The can filled, heaped up, but Ricardo still poured, slowly. Then when the first berry fell off, he stopped. That was one unit. The workers were paid according to the number of cans they had picked, and if someone had half a can left over, they would set it apart to be counted in with the next day's picking.

And there stood Adela. She had never been to school a day in her life. She could not read. She could not write. But she could figure! If she could have paid everybody for the amount they picked each day, she would not have seemed such a mathematical wizard, but some of the servants were paid ten pesos, or twenty pesos in advance; some were paid only after several days of picking. And Adela kept the accounts in her head with no help of pencil or paper.

Awed by her feat I asked, "Does anybody ever try to cheat you?"

"Oh, yes," she answered. "When we are measuring they will say to me, 'That makes seven cans,' and I say to them, 'No, that is five cans.'" She chuckled and then without bragging but completely confident she added, "My head knows."

The coffee pickers furnished us with a ready-made congregation for our teaching. While they waited their turn, or after they had been paid, most of them, at one time or another, dropped by our house. Sometimes Helen played the Mazatec records that had been made by Gospel Recordings when George Cowan took Tomás into Mexico City. Sometimes she showed them the Gospel nut with its colored ribbon.

Usually just before dusk she pulled her portable organ out into the middle of the room and started to play. She had been doing that ever since arriving in Río Sancho and anywhere from ten to twenty people, most of them young fellows, were in the habit of gathering. Some leaned against the wall, some sat on one of our two long benches. We passed out the hymnbooks to them all, even to those who could not read.

To help them to learn, I turned their books right

side up and found the page for them. Then with
a hymnbook of my own I sat where the people could
see and pointed to the words with my pencil. The
men held their books very properly while they slyly
peeked out from under their hats and watched my
pencil go back and forth across the page.

At first they had no idea how to find the hymn
selected. When I said, "We will sing page 1 now,"
they might turn to the middle or to the back of
the book. After awhile this person and then that
one discovered that the book went in sequence, and
that they could find any one of the thirty-five hymns
if they counted the pages.

One of those who came to sing every night was
an eight-year-old girl. She was a cute little thing,
just getting over the toothless stage. Every time we
sang a different song, I found the place for her.
All at once she caught on to the counting system
and she poked me in the ribs with, "Look! Look! I
found it." A little later she said, "I can find them
now. I am thinking."

"Umph!" said a man across the circle. "That
must be because you have got door-teeth." I had
never heard that word "door-teeth" before, but it
was apparent that he was reminding her that she
had just acquired her permanent teeth and that she
was not as smart as she thought she was. The little
girl kept still after that, but her eyes were shining.

The men were in the habit of requesting their
favorite hymns and some of them we would sing
two or three times an evening. Every once in awhile
we would stop singing and memorize a Bible verse
together, or I would tell a Bible story. One night

I called on one of the young fellows to pray. He had never prayed in public before, so as he prayed, eyes closed, he nervously twisted his book round and round. When we started to sing again, his book was upside down. He turned the pages frantically but nothing looked right. I switched his book around for him and glanced up in time to see his pal across the circle quietly chuckling at his predicament.

Lino's younger brother, Daniel, took an active part in those gatherings. When there was too much rowdiness, he would call, "Quiet, boys, she is telling us what God says!" Or after I had finished telling them that Jesus Christ died in our behalf and then arose again he would look around sternly and say, "Believe, fellows! It is the truth she is saying." Sometimes in his earnestness, he would reteach the lesson, and he did it very well.

I liked it when the lessons were retaught. For one thing there was no real beginning to the meetings, and some of the people drifted in so late they would have missed the point entirely if we had not gone back over it.

Most everyone was very polite about their comings and goings—too polite. They shook hands all the way around each time. Helen became clever at sticking out her left hand for a touch on the finger tips while playing on with her right. No one bothered to wait for the end of the hymn, but neither would he exclude the organist from his salutation.

For the most part their departures were dependent on how far each was from home. Every evening they discussed the clouds, the stars, the moon, and argued about how soon it would get dark. Some would have to pass fierce dogs on the way home. All had rocky trails. None of them liked the dark, so each judged the night and stayed as long as he could. When the moment came, he turned in his hymnbook, shook hands with the rest of us, and went out the door, often with an exclamation at the darkness.

One young boy solved the problem by carrying a candle. He used to leave early but, now he had his candle, he sat back with a little smile while the others rushed to the door to watch the night. Then when we closed the meeting, he would put his hand around the flame, protecting it from wind or fog, and make his way up the crooked mountain path.

One evening at the close, just as Helen was shutting the organ, a drunken man walked in, followed by a fellow in a bright blue shirt. Drunken men had been there before, but they had been harmless, talking foolishly. This fellow was ready to pick a fight. "Sing a song!" he said. "I've got the police with me, and I want you to sing a song."

Without the organ I started one of the more familiar ones, and the other people joined in with me. The man was quiet as long as we sang, but when we were done he snarled, "Sing me a pretty song. One with the machine the way you are supposed to!" I suggested he come back the next evening, because we had finished for the day. "Well, come on, then!" he said to the others. "Let's go!" Not a man stirred. They did not want to be on the trail with him.

"Go along by yourself," they told him, "we're not going your way." Then Blue Shirt got up, took him by the arm, and the two went out together.

I might not have discovered who Blue Shirt was if I had not been working at the never-ending task of language study. Frequently I would ask one of my visitors, "What have you been doing today?" And I would write down his answer, urging him to go into detail, because the longer the story, the more language material he was giving me. Then I would study what I had written, for new words, idioms, or some quirk in the grammar that I had not known about.

One day I asked a young fellow the usual question, and his answer was very matter-of-fact. "I just put a man in jail. He was drunk. He beat his wife. It will cost him twenty pesos to get out." That was the first I knew that it was the police I had been entertaining. The drunken man, who a few nights before had insisted that we sing, had been right. He did have the police with him. Blue Shirt was one of them, and many of the young fellows who came to sing were on the force too. That explained why they were able to stay until eight o'clock—they were all on night duty.

Blue Shirt turned up frequently after that. Many times he would have someone with him who had not heard the Gospel records, or who had not been at the meetings. One evening as we were singing, someone threw a stone at our door. It landed with a thud. Instantly the fellows were on the alert. "Who did that?"

"A drunk!"

"Let's put him in jail!" said Nono, one of the more boisterous ones.

"Oh, no," said Blue Shirt and called for another hymn. Even as we sang, I prayed for him, wondering if he was one of the future leaders of the Mazatec church.

A few evenings later while the fellows were listening to a lesson from the Bible, there was a sudden sharp attention-getting whistle from outside. It was followed by the measured notes of whistle-talk. Every man in the place put down his book and hurried to the door. One of them picked up our heavy door-stick as he went. Outside they were greeted with a hoot of laughter from those who had whistled. I had not understood the whistle-talk, so was at a loss to know what had happened. One of the boys translated for me. "They said a poisonous snake was about to enter the house."

Everyone knew that a snake could enter anywhere between the ground and the bottom of the board wall, and the fellows had acted accordingly. The ones who had whistled were pleased with the success of their joke and took special delight in the boy who had picked up the door-stick for a weapon.

Nono had been in on that joke, but even as he was teasing the others, he himself entered and reached for a hymnbook. He liked to sing, and he persisted until he could read the whole hymnbook.

One day while he was in the house looking at magazines, a drunken man came to the window. The man had heard that we "knew God," and he asked me to tell him about Him. I did not want to turn him away, but neither did I want to talk with him too long when he was in that condition. I handed a hymnbook to Nono and said, "You tell him."

"Sure," said Nono. Page by page he went through, reading the hymns and giving a word of explanation with each. I sat across the room, supposedly reading, but actually listening, happy that another Mazatec was able and willing to tell a fellow tribesman about the Lord.

The drunken man left, and a few minutes later Blue Shirt arrived. He sat on the bench beside Nono, and they both were quiet as they turned the pages of their magazines. All at once Nono stood up, cursed, and punched Blue Shirt in the forehead. I had glanced up at the curse and was in time to see Blue Shirt's head snap back. It whammed against the wall with a thud. Blue Shirt was not interested in fighting. He kept his seat and asked softly, "What's the matter?"

"I heard what you said!"

"I did not say anything."

From across the room I asked, "What did he say?"

"He knows what he said!" (I never did find out what got into Nono that day. I really believe that Blue Shirt had not said anything.) "Stand up and fight!" Nono snarled.

Again I spoke. "No fighting here." Nono lowered his fist. It always amazed me that I was able to enforce my rule of no fighting inside the house. If they had gone ahead and fought I do not know what I could have done about it, but so far our house had remained neutral territory. I tried to be peacemaker, but I was not successful. Nono could not persuade Blue Shirt to go outside and fight, so finally he left with a contemptuous, "Are you a woman?"

He kept watch on the house, and when Blue Shirt left, he followed him. Out in front of the store, with a circle of fellows looking on, he beat him up. The judge ordered that both of them be put in jail for fighting, but, since the jail consisted of just one room, Nono was put in first. After he had served his time, Blue Shirt was locked up.

Nono had come out nonchalant, and self-confident as ever, but being in jail shamed and distressed Blue Shirt. His sentence was only for two days, but he broke out. That made him a fugitive. He left town, and went into hiding down in the lowlands. Sometime later we heard that he had died of malaria down there.

CHAPTER XVIII

Lino's Household

(SPRING OF 1946)

DURING THE COFFEE SEASON the people of Río Sancho were busy from early morning until late afternoon. One of their jobs was getting the half-dried coffee out into the sun. Lino and one of the hired men carried the heavy bags into the yard, and Adela or the children spread it out. Then usually Lino went on to the coffee groves while the rest of the family stayed to watch the drying coffee. It was the children's job to keep the chickens out of it. "No, they do not eat it," they told me, "but while they are scratching for bugs, they scatter it all over."

Adela kept her eye on the clouds, and when rain seemed close, she and the children swept up the coffee. Sometimes rain came without much warning. Then Helen and I heard the shouts, the running feet, the hurried scrape of broom or board, and we would go out to help.

Once after such a scramble I decided to rest on the stalk of a banana tree, but while I was still in mid-air, Lino shouted. I managed to reverse direction, feeling rather foolish and wondering what the trouble was. He explained that the juice from the banana tree stained, and Adela added, "You would have scrubbed your dress until the cloth disappeared before that stain came out."

That spoiled a number of potential seats. In several places around the yard, the more recently picked coffee was piled in heaps, and the berries were kept within bounds by the stumps of the banana trees with which they were banked up.

Coffee was so plentiful that year that Lino was having trouble. He used every square foot of space, spreading the coffee from the wall of their house to the wall of ours, but there still was not enough level land for all of it.

One morning instead of going out with the coffee pickers, he stayed home and set the hired men digging at the bank and breaking rock with dynamite. After awhile I went out to watch and he started talking. "I have to have more level land because I have to get the coffee dry. If I do not, I cannot pay the servants. If I do not pay the servants, they do not eat. They have not any money. They have not coffee of their own. All they have is what I give them." Actually he was no more educated than they were. He knew no Spanish. But because of his drive, he was one of the first of the area, five years later, to bring in a machine that cut the flesh off the coffee bean. Because it lessened the drying time, the coffee came out a better quality, and not as much level land was needed.

Daniel was Lino's mouthpiece. That is, his Spanish mouthpiece and his Spanish ears. Lino made the decisions, but any business with the outside world went through Daniel. Since he was accustomed to thinking about words and language, Daniel was a good one to help check the typed copy of the Gospel of Mark that Florrie had sent over.

He worked with the coffee in good weather, but for an hour or two on most rainy days, I listened while he read the Gospel of Mark aloud. He read in Mazatec quite easily, but the important thing was he thought while he read, and he was quick to say if a word was not right, or if there was something he did not understand.

He read through 1:6: "And John was clothed with camel's hair, and with a girdle of skin about his loins; and he did eat locusts and wild honey." He studied the verse awhile, then he looked up and asked, "Whose land was the honey on?"

How did I know? I sputtered a bit and finally said, "Those bees were not in a box near someone's house. Those bees were in a tree out in the wilds."

He was not satisfied. "I have land. It was my father's. It is land way out where no one is, and it has bees on it." And then he asked again, "On whose land was the honey that John ate?"

I admitted, "I do not know whose land it was. It was probably not his own."

Then Daniel put his brown finger on one word in the Mazatec script. "Then this is not right. This says that John owned the land."

I was learning so much working with Daniel that I would have liked to have worked eight hours a day until we had finished Mark. But I guess life in a tribe is never like that. Language work and translation are the backdrop, always present but sometimes ignored while the actors claim attention.

The lives of our neighbors affected ours as we

became friends and tried to teach them of the Lord.
We had an interest and curiosity about their way of
doing things. Perhaps that is why we were so quick
to notice when Adela was missing. The people had
gathered while Ricardo measured their loads, but
it was Lino, not Adela, who was cashier. That is
queer, we thought, and wondered how he managed
without her mental notes.

The next morning Glafira walked up to the door
of our house but when she saw that we had visitors
she went on by. She was Lino's sister-in-law. Her
husband owned land next to Lino's and the two
families worked together. A little later she was
back, but it was not until her third try that she
found us alone. Inside she whispered, "Lino has
another wife."

I heard the words but my mind refused to understand them. "Another animal—a mule?" I asked—
there was a slight similarity between the two words.

"No! A woman! He had Adela but now he has
another."

Oh! I had known that Mazatec men did that.
Two wives were quite common with the well-to-do
men, and usually they did it for one of two reasons.
If the first wife had no children, they took a second
wife in the hope that they would have children by
her. Or if they needed more help in the kitchen,
they took another wife instead of a maid. That was
the reason Lino had done it. Adela could not be
cashier and grind corn at the same time. Perhaps
she could have managed for her husband and children, but the hired men expected to be fed too.

Glafira told us that the second wife's name was

Ofelia, and that Lino had paid her parents the marriage price for her. He had gone after her and brought her home the previous afternoon.

That was why Adela had not been out paying the coffee pickers. She was angry and unhappy, and Lino had to do the job himself. He had other troubles brought on by Adela's anger. It made him concerned for their six-month-old son. According to the Mazatecs the milk of an angry mother is apt to make her baby sick, so Lino hired a witch doctor to try to prevent it.

From our house across the yard we could hear the witch doctor's rhythmical chant. It went one, two, three, four, *five,* six. His night was divided up in sections about ten or fifteen minutes long. He started each section shouting loudly and in a high pitch. Gradually he lowered both the pitch and the loudness of his voice until all I could hear was a rumbling growl. Whether loud or soft he never changed the speed or rhythm, it remained one, two, three, four, *five,* six.

Not only did he go from loud to soft each ten-minute section, but he also controlled the interval from his loudest shout to his softest mumble. At the start of the evening his loudest shout was never very loud, and his mumble was almost inaudible. Gradually he increased the volume of each section until by midnight, the high point, he was shouting. After midnight the volume of his chant gradually decreased until by sunrise it was mostly a mumble and inaudible.

In the evening the first words I had caught had been, "Come with the wind. Come with the clouds.

Wind is present, clouds are present." A little later
I heard, "Shut it off with rock. Shut it off with a
bottomless pit." When he started shouting again he
was calling on Father Sun, Father Moon, and the
Virgin Mary. They too were supposed to shut off
something with a bottomless pit.

Later he called to the saints. "Come here, Saint.
Come here, San Antonio, San Pablo, San Pedro.
Come here. Come here, Holy Mary. There is no
death, there is no trouble. Let there be death. Let
there be trouble."

Apparently that was all just the preliminary. He
finally got down to the business of the night. He
called on the saints again and then, "Let the baby
get fat." Mumble, mumble and I could not hear.
Lying in bed, I tried to take down the words of his
chant by the light of a flashlight. I did pretty well
around midnight when he was shouting loudest, but
as the night progressed I could get only the louder
shouts at the beginning of each section. As dawn
neared I could not even hear the louder parts, and
I lay down again to sleep.

By midmorning the whole town knew that Lino
had taken another wife. A number of the women
found an excuse to call on us, in order to watch the
house across the yard. While they were there, Lino's
six-year-old daughter came in. Just a glance at her
told me that she was miserable and unhappy, but
my guests had no mercy. "So your father has another woman."

No answer.

"I'll bet your mother is mad."

"That is not so; my mother is happy." She lied loyally and ran out almost in tears.

The women had almost forgotten my existence. They had not come to see me anyway, so they began to discuss the affair paying no attention to me. "It is a clear case of . . ." What was that word? I did not move, but I listened closely. For years we had wondered how to say "adultery" and "fornication." We needed it in John 8:4 and Mark 10:11. Was that the word they had used? The women went on. "That Lino is just a pig, and he is . . ." There was the same basic word, but this time in the form of a verb. Quietly I reached for a pencil and wrote it down. Lino's deed was a high price to pay for it, but at last we had the word we needed.

Eventually Adela decided to accept the situation and went back to measuring coffee and paying the workers. Lino carried on his family responsibilities and comforted his daughter by gently hunting through her hair for lice. She beamed as he did it, and her smiles came easily again.

The family was quieting, but what about us? What should our attitude be? I was puzzled. We could not undo what had been done. As I thought over the sequence of events, I remembered that there were occasions when a man had loved the Lord, even while having plural wives; King David had done so. And I remembered too that John 16:9 implies that the worst sin is disbelief in the Lord. So I decided that at least my heaviest emphasis would be on the sin of trusting witchcraft instead of the Lord.

Ofelia stayed inside the house, apparently too

bashful to be seen. When I finally got a glimpse of her, she was a nice-looking girl, and I guessed her to be about twenty years old. Adela had begun treating her like a daughter-in-law, ordering her around in the same kindly way she ordered the servants—that of course being the way a daughter-in-law was treated.

Then one day Adela, Glafira, and Ofelia all came to call. It was a semiofficial visit, by which they were notifying us that Ofelia was part of the family now. In our house the other two ignored her—did not speak to her, did not speak about her. She just sat there, while the rest of us chatted away. I had been ironing, and Adela picked up one of my tatted handkerchiefs and admired it. After she was through examining it, I walked over and handed it to Ofelia so that she could look at it too. Adela smiled and things relaxed. I had recognized Ofelia as one of them.

A few days later Helen and I were singing and Adela heard us. She called to Ofelia, "Go in and sing. You will like it." Ofelia did not want to come. She gave the excuse that the door of their house was open. No one left his house open in those parts. If he did, dogs were apt to go in and steal lard or whatever else they could get their noses into. But Adela still urged her with, "I will watch the house. Go on." So Ofelia came in and heard for the first time about the Lord.

CHAPTER XIX

Others Too

(FALL OF 1946)

WE ALWAYS HATED LEAVING the tribe even for such a worthy cause as teaching at the Summer Institute of Linguistics, but one part of that I found to be advantageous. It gave us the opportunity to view our work from a distance, and the chance to start with a slightly different point of view in the fall. As I stood back and looked at the past year in Río Sancho, it seemed to me that our energies had been too confined to Lino's household and to the people who had the initiative to call on us. It seemed to me that we needed to get out to the other families of Río Sancho.

People at home called us pioneers, but we were not pioneers just because we had left the States and gone to Mexico, nor because we had gone from Mexico City to Chalco, and from Chalco to Río Sancho. I was finding that we could sit in the middle of an untouched village with people receptive and anxious to hear about Christ and still reach only one family. Of course it was a large family by the time you added the servants, school children, some of the relatives, and the police, but I was concerned for the women of Río Sancho.

The path that went by our house was one of the main thoroughfares of the village, made so by the fact that "clean water" was just beyond. The people of Río Sancho did have an idea of sanitation and there was a village agreement that all washing of clothes, watering of animals, bathing, etc., should be done below a certain point. Above that point was "clean water" and no one was supposed to contaminate it.

Women were constantly passing our house with their water jugs. In their curiosity they would stop and look in our window, but they seldom had the courage to come all the way in. I decided that the next step was to witness to those women.

It was not easy. They would stop to watch us, or to ask for a tin can, but the minute we tried to talk seriously, off they would dash. Finally I decided to make up a song especially for the women. I had discovered that they did not run from a hymn, but the present hymns did not satisfy me. I needed one that would tell, as clearly as speech would have done, that the Lord loved them, that He had died in their behalf, but that He arose again.

The tune I chose was "Jesus Saves." It took awhile to make the message fit the music. In fact, in at least one place I had to change the music to fit the words, but at last it was done. And it worked!

Several of the women learned to sing it, and they all liked to hear it. Sometimes I would sing a line and then stop and talk about it, sing another line and talk some more. Queer how music held them while other things frightened them away!

But hearing a song now and then was not enough.

They needed lessons from the Bible; they needed to read Scripture verses and Bible stories for themselves. I decided that I would go to their homes and teach them there. Marion Doble went with me. She did not know the language well enough to make contact with a new family easily, but after we had called a few times together, she could carry on.

The first place we went was just down the road a way. From the path I shouted, "Hello, hello, we have come to see you." Two sisters were in the kitchen working. They invited us in and after we had exchanged a few commonplaces, I came to the point. "Wouldn't you like to know paper? See I have a book here."

"Oh," said they, "you have a book." With that much encouragement I went over and squatted on the floor beside one of the sisters. She was kneeling beside the fire tending the corncakes that the other was grinding. Smoke got in my eyes from the fire, and my knees got wet from the damp dirt floor. As I turned the pages, I waxed enthusiastic over the clowns, birds, and the people that were shown in the primer. But not a spark of encouragement did I get from them. One of the women gestured to the heap of corn. "Are we unoccupied that we should have time to read? We have work. Let the children study."

At the second house the woman was too startled to even invite us inside, but I slid the primer under her nose anyway. She protested, "Let the children learn; they are young, and their heads are still soft. I am old and my head is hard."

"You can learn; I know you can." I pointed to a picture, "What do you suppose this is?"

"It looks like a boy."

"That is right. And here is where it says *boy*. If you study, soon you will be able to read everything this book says. Tomorrow we will come again, and then we will study, shall we?"

"I have no time. I have a husband. Men must eat. Men must have their clothes washed. She who has a husband has work."

"Yes, I know, but you could study a little while every day."

"Well, maybe."

We did not need more permission than that. The next day we were back, and that time we were invited inside and given chairs. The whole family was home and it was apparent that the woman had been talking about our previous visit. Everyone knew why we had come, and they immediately gathered around. But they had also made up their minds who I was going to teach. Almost before I knew what was happening, I found myself teaching the father. Without too much trouble, but with great pride, he read through the first section. I was delighted but a little chagrined. After all it was the women I had intended to teach in those daily excursions.

There just were not hours enough in the day to teach everybody I wanted to, nor were there days enough. Word came from our director in Mexico City that I was to help two girls get started in the Mixtec tribe. He thought I was the logical one to

send, because that was the tribe where my brother
Ken had been working. I had never been there, and
the language was completely different from Mazatec, but the director thought I might enjoy seeing
the places I had heard about.

My job was to help the new translators as they
traveled in a country strange to them, make the necessary contacts with the town government, and set
up supply lines for food.

All that was in the line of duty, but there was
something extra I was doing just for the fun of it.
I staged a race between "youth" and "science."
The contestants were I, as I was in 1936—young—
and I, as I was in 1946—with experience and linguistic know-how. If I could learn the Mixtec language faster in 1946 that I had learned Mazatec in
1936, then "science" would win. If I could not, then
"youth" would win.

While the girls were memorizing words and sentences, so was I. While they walked around drilling
themselves with flash cards, so did I. Talking and
understanding Mixtec was a struggle, but by the
time the month was ended there was no question
but what science had won.

After the girls had made friends, and had learned
enough language to get on by themselves, I went
back to Mexico City. While I was there, packing
and buying supplies for Chalco, I learned that the
long-hoped-for thing had happened. A Gospel was
in print for the Mazatecs. It was not the Gospel of
John. While that book had been delayed, Florrie
had pushed ahead with the Gospel of Mark. That
was the one that was just off the press. Copies had

not even gone out to Chalco yet. Florrie and George, and all of us were waiting to use them, so I put some copies in my saddlebag and took them out special delivery. My comment at the time could be summarized in "Yippee!" and "Praise the Lord!" But Florrie did better. At Christmas time she reminded us that we were celebrating both the "birth of the Incarnate Word and the birth of the Written Word for the Mazatecs."

Every day in Río Sancho we would read a portion of the Gospel of Mark during the evening gatherings. Then I would question the people about what we had read, and retell the parts that they had missed. The next evening I would explain a new portion and Helen or one of the men would review the previous portion.

I was amazed at how satisfying the Gospel of Mark was. Some of our lessons were: Mark 2:13-17, Christ came to save sinners; Mark 3:31-35, we are children of God and brothers of one another; Mark 4:2-9, 11-20, we should tell others of Christ, even if we do not know how people will react; Mark 7:1-9, 18-23, a Christian should have a clean life, he should not commit adultery; Mark 7:24-30, Christ is stronger than the demons.

It was after that meeting that one of the men said to me, "I have seen an evil spirit." I did not react.

"I have!" Silence.

"Do you believe me when I say I have seen an evil spirit?" Well, I was willing to listen.

Celia thought she had seen an evil spirit too. She told of the time she had awakened in the middle of the night and saw a skeleton standing by the fire.

She was frightened; she was concerned for her husband Rafael. People had been threatening him for some time, and she thought that someone must have hired a witch doctor to cast a spell on him. When she read of Christ's power, she was comforted, and she and Rafael began to study the Bible regularly.

In answer to their question about plural wives, I told the story of Abraham. "Abraham got tired of waiting for Sarah to have a son, so he took the maid. The maid had a son, but God told Abraham that He would not fulfill His promises through that one; it had to be through Sarah's son. Later the descendants of the maid caused trouble for the descendants of the first wife."

"That tells us," said Rafael. "It always causes trouble when a man has more than one wife."

Glafira's husband was reading too. He was the one who took the Gospel of Mark to the fields and read while the goats were feeding. According to Glafira, he "read the entire book through almost every day." I doubted that, but at least from somewhere he picked up the names "Scribe" and "Pharisee" for his two mischievous children. He also was the one who paraphrased Mark 2:9 in his morning greeting. He would say, "It is late; pick up your bed and walk."

In a small way the Gospel of Mark was already becoming part of their lives.

CHAPTER XX

Helpers

(Spring of 1947)

THE MEN AND BOYS had been learning to read pretty well, but the teaching of the women was still going at a snail's pace. Our director in Mexico City decided to send four girls out to help us. None of them knew Mazatec, but they had all had linguistic training at the Summer Institute of Linguistics, and we hoped that it would not be long before they could teach the women.

They were hardly rested from their travel before I took them up to see the girl who had been helping me as language informant. She was pleased at the opportunity to study the strangers more closely and was patient while they mimicked her and practiced pronunciation of Mazatec.

They drilled the polite things people say when they meet, and the things they say when they leave. They practiced reading the primers and singing the hymns. Actually singing the hymns was easier than reading, because in singing they could follow the tune of the hymn and ignore the tone marks that indicated the pitch of the spoken word. Within a week they were ready to start teaching.

We decided to divide the village up into sections.

Each of the new girls would take a road and teach the people who lived along that road. I was not to have any steady pupils; my job was to help the new girls get started—and I would not have very long to do that because our director had written to tell me that I was to be lent to the Zapotec tribe for two months.

Each morning one of the new girls and I walked through one section of town. In the afternoon another girl and I took a different section. We stopped at each house and tried to persuade the people to learn to read. Most of the men were away working, but usually there was at least one woman at home, and sometimes she was willing to try.

The teaching conditions were very seldom ideal. More typical was the home in which Meg Geiger taught. The woman sat on a mat on the floor while on a six-inch stool beside her Meg had to hold the book out of the reach of the year-old baby that sometimes aimlessly whacked and pulled on his mother. A three-year-old boy insisted on seeing whatever it was his mother was looking at, and as he did so his big straw hat blocked off her view of the page. An eight-year-old daughter was not interested in reading, but her overwhelming curiosity about other things kept her interrupting with, "How much did your dress cost?" or "What is this for?"

In spite of all the difficulties, the women learned something, and after each lesson Meg, or whoever was teaching, sang a hymn with the family. The recently translated "Jesus Saves" became a great favorite, and soon it was being sung all over town.

Probably some of the women endured the reading lessons for the privilege of singing afterward.

Once the people found out that we were going to the different homes to teach, some of them hunted us out. I was with Iris Mills one morning when some children led us to their home. We hardly had time to greet the people before they told us, "We do not want to study reading, we want to hear about God." Then they pointed to an older woman sitting in the middle of the room. "She is the one who wants to hear."

The woman moved her mat and sat at our feet. Her children, grandchildren and neighbors crowded around. We sang and explained and sang some more. When the children talked while we were singing, their grandmother said sternly, "Keep still and listen."

The woman's grown son came in, and soon he asked, "Have those words been written?" We pointed out the hymnbook, and, his hands trembling with excitement, he took it. He could read a little, and he watched the words while we sang "God Will Take Care of You."

I told him, "I will sell you this book for twenty centavos."

"You will?" He began to shout. "Twenty centavos! Money! Where is the money? Someone give her twenty centavos." Several of the family looked in different nooks, but no one could find any money. Finally someone went next door and brought back the needed amount.

They gave me the money and I handed the man the book. Then the question came up as to where the book should be kept—in the house of the man who could read, or in the house of the person who had supplied the money. After considerable discussion they decided that the man could keep the book, but he was to read it to the others.

We were not ten feet from the door of that house before a woman slipped up and said softly, "Come to my house." She led us up a narrow path to a house we would never have found by ourselves, and a group of six women were there waiting for us.

I had not guessed that people would be so friendly and so anxious to hear. And I was thrilled that the girls who had been in the tribe just two or three weeks could teach them. Of course they were very limited in subject matter, but they could help them to read, teach them the hymns, and read them Bible verses. If the people wanted their questions answered, they had to ask someone who had been in the tribe longer. For the most part the people were gracious and appreciative of the effort the girls were making. When they jumbled their words, the people tried to understand them anyway. When I remarked on their patience one of the women said to me, "It is our language you are talking. If we do not understand you, that is our fault."

George Cowan came over for five days each week to help us in our concentrated effort to teach the people of Río Sancho. He did not take a section of town like the girls had done, but when a man stayed home with a sore foot, or for some similar reason, George took over the visitation of that home. In that way he did most of the teaching of the men and they of the women.

I was proud of the girls and the way they went out, rain or shine, mostly rain. When the trails were wet, the clay earth was slippery, and walking at such times was difficult. One day Ethel Wallis and I slipped and slid as we went after clean water. We were coming back, walking very carefully, carrying the water in a five-gallon can between us. The can had a stick across the top of it, and I was holding one side and she was holding the other. When we were almost home, we had to cross a log bridge. The bridge was rather narrow for the two of us with the can between, and just as we reached the middle of it Ethel slipped. Rather than pull me in with her, she let go of the can, then over she went. Splash! The water was not more than two feet deep, but she fell in such a way that she went completely under. She had not hit any rocks and in a second she stood up laughing.

Some of the children who lived nearby did not wait to help, they did not even wait to laugh, they ran directly to the house where the other girls were and announced, "Ethel is dead!"

From their point of view she was as good as dead because they believed that she had insulted demons who inhabit the water. They expected that she would develop a fever, lose weight, and slowly die. They said that because she had insulted the water spirit she would dry up.

Ethel was none the worse for her fall, and it gave us a chance to explain that we did not know anything about water spirits, but we did know that Christ is stronger than demons, and if they were there, we were depending on Him for protection.

The family who had seen her fall listened carefully and kept their eyes on Ethel.

A month passed. She was still in good health. The man of the family commented, "If that had been one of us, we would be dead."

I remembered his remark a year later when a teen-age boy died. Catarina told me that he had been helping to build a bridge across the river at the foot of the Chalco mountain. Something happened and he fell into the water. There was a doctor in Chalco at the time, but in spite of all he could do, the boy died three weeks later.

"Had he hit his head on a rock?" I asked.

"No."

"Did he get a cold?"

"No."

"Why did he die?"

"He was frightened." I questioned other people too, and some of them said that he had insulted the water spirits.

I had known of only one person whose death had been attributed to that reason, but the family who lived by the bridge in Río Sancho knew of several. Therefore when their own little daughter fell in, they were very concerned.

We were not in town when it happened, but afterward they told us that her big sister pulled her out, and her mother spanked her until she breathed again. But even though the little girl had no bruises, and though she ate a good lunch, the family was frightened.

Then they remembered Ethel Wallis. She had fallen into the water with a splash, but she had not died. We had said that she would not die, and they discussed the reasons we gave. As they remembered, they took courage. That night they instructed the little girl, "Pray to Jesus. Tell Him that you want Him to protect you from the water spirits." So the little girl prayed, and the family slept that night.

But the neighbors knew she had fallen, and they were watching for signs of her drying up. It made the little girl nervous and once in awhile she cried. Then her mother would say, "Do not be frightened. Remember Ethel is alive to this day. Pray again to Jesus, He will take care of you."

The little girl did not die, and when her mother told me of their experience, I thanked the Lord that He had let Ethel have a ducking that day.

CHAPTER XXI

Moving Day

(SPRING OF 1947, FALL OF 1947)

I HAD NOT BEEN ABLE to stay in Río Sancho as long as the four helpers did that spring. Our director in Mexico City sent word that I was to be lent to the Zapotec tribe for two months. Margaret Hull, one of the girls who had been teaching reading, went with me. With her help I made progress on the Mazatec even while I was not in the tribe. She learned to read my handwriting and managed to type up a "verb file," culling regular and irregular verbs from an old notebook and from a previous file whose alphabet was out of date. The file included the "principal parts" of each irregular verb and gave a sample of each type of the regular verbs. In the evenings she asked me questions about anything that had puzzled her, but except for that she worked alone.

While she was working on the verb file, I was listening to an informant and trying to write tone on the Zapotec words that Otis and Mary Leal had given me. They had already spelled the words correctly, so I did not have to pay any attention to the ordinary letters, but even listening for tone and ignoring all else just about cracked my ear. The tone of the individual words was not always the same. In fact, they changed in a most confusing fashion. My job was to find the system within which those changes were made. Sometimes I doubted that I would ever find it, but I kept on working—that was what I had gone out there for.

Mary said that she could tell the progress I was making, even while standing at a distance, by listening to the adjectives with which I described the language. The order of progression went something like this: "Horrible!" "Mean!" "Amazing!" "Fascinating!" "Simple!" "Boring!"

Amazing crept in when I began to suspect the answer. *Fascinating* was the answer when I found it. *Simple* was Zapotec once it was analyzed. *Boring* was the tedious job of following through. But every so often *simple* reverted to *horrible* as I found I had been making a mistake.

I wrote letters to Ken telling him my troubles and triumphs, and he answered with suggestions and advice. His letters were helpful, but best of all, he himself came. He agreed with my analysis, and then he helped me write up a paper describing it. We did not stay in Zapotec territory to finish it, because all of us were on staff at the Summer Institute of Linguistics. My main job was teaching, but I managed to work on the paper too. It was ready for publication before the course was over, and I was delighted that I could go back to Río Sancho knowing that at least one thing had been "finished" that year.

Some other things were not giving that satisfied feeling. Our life in Río.Sancho was rather upset because Lino had said that he needed the house in which we had been living. We could have moved back to Chalco, but we did not want to. We hoped that more of the people in Río Sancho might learn to read the Gospel. Hoping to stay, I asked several people to rent us their house, but none of them thought they could.

Meg was with me at that time, and we started to pack for Chalco. We put in one corner those things that are handy in an Indian village, but which were not worth carrying out. By the time we had them all together, old magazines, bottles, tin cans, and little boxes, it made quite a heap.

I stopped in the middle of packing to call on Celia. She was disappointed when she heard that we were leaving, and she suggested a family that might be willing to rent to us. The husband was away from home when I asked about the house, but his wife sent for him, and in less than two hours we had his permission. I was almost jubilant. Each time someone had turned us down, the more I knew I wanted to stay. By the time the man had agreed to rent to us, even the task of moving did not seem bad.

Meg and I did not know what we would do, however, since none of the men wanted to take time off from their regular work, and there were no pack animals available. Our inquiries let the boys of the village know that something unusual was going on, and they gathered to watch. Soon our house was teeming with nine-, ten-, and eleven-year-old boys. Well, even those small bodies could perform a lot of work if the energy in them was harnessed. We decided to make small loads and let the boys carry for us.

"Me! Me!" they shouted, pushing and jostling for a position in which to receive a load. They waited until each had his, then they walked or ran up the road together. I stayed in our old house packing, and Meg went up to the new house to receive.

The boys took four trips and then they quit. "We are tired," they said. "We are not going to carry any more." I paid them with Christmas cards for the work they had done, and then I understood why they had stopped. They wanted to see what kind of pay they were getting. Once they knew, they started working again.

The next time I paid them with magazines. They sat and compared books, decided whose was the best, and then asked for another load.

The little girls felt left out because I was giving the boys all the prizes. They had begged to be allowed to carry, but I thought that the loads were too heavy for them. Then about noon the boys went on a complete—and what appeared to be— a final strike. Not knowing what else to do, I broke the loads up into even smaller sizes and gave them to the eight-, nine-, and ten-year-old girls. By that time all the paper things were gone from the heap of give-away-ables, and I began to pay with bottles. The boys could not stand having the girls win them all, and with a rush they were back on duty.

Finally only big things were left. I told my little helpers that everything else was too heavy. A man would have to carry the rest. The boys looked at the bottles in the corner and figured out a way to get more. They decided that two of them could carry a big box together. That started it. They would test a box, and according to its weight, one, two, or three of them carried it.

Six of them got under the kitchen table and away they went, squealing and yelling with excitement. When they came to the bridge, it was narrower than the table, and they had an engineering problem, but they made it.

By that time some of the bigger boys came to the door and they wanted bottles too. "Oh, no," I told them, "these bottles are just for the workers." Two of them complied by carrying a trunk between them.

I noticed that everyone who had tested one certain box left it for someone else to carry. It was a kerosene box packed with books. My supply of bottles was running low, but I picked out the biggest and best bottle and put it in my pocket. When the children saw and asked for it, I told them, "I am saving this bottle for the one who carries that box over there."

At last everything had gone but that one box. The children looked at each other, at me, at the box, at the bottle in my pocket. We rested for awhile that way. Then Nono appeared. "Carry this last box for me, will you?" I asked him. His pals cheered as he went over and picked up one corner. Immediately he dropped it with a whistle of protest. I agreed that it was heavy and asked if he was strong enough. He did not answer, but while at least twenty of us looked on, he adjusted the carrying rope. Satisfied, he slung the box over his shoulder and with a whoop he was off. I picked up the broom, shut the door, and we all followed.

Meg had been working hard at the receiving end, piling up kerosene boxes for "kitchen cupboards," making "chests of drawers" out of more boxes, placing utensils in the proper places. But our possessions had arrived in such tiny bunches that much of it was still a jumbled mess. We could not straighten it out that night; we hunted until we found food for supper, dug out some bedding, and moved things here and there until we had space enough to set up our cots.

The house was plenty big, but we did not have full possession of it yet. We had moved so fast that the family had not had time to get all their things out. They had put their belongings at one end of the house and had strung up two sheets between that section of the house and the part that was ready for our use.

I wondered what they had left there, but neither Meg nor I looked behind the curtain. I climbed into bed, as exhausted as the children who had carried for us should have been.

I do not know how long I had been sleeping, and I do not know how many times Meg had called, but finally I heard her. She was whispering softly but urgently, "Eunice."

I did not want to wake up but I managed to say, "Mm?"

"There is a man behind the curtain!"

What should I do? Maybe I should have gotten up. At that time of night I felt too tired to move or even think—so I did not. Taking the lazy way out, I said, "Get in bed with me."

Meg did, but my sleep was not peaceful after that. I listened and I could hear the man breathing and turning on his bed. He was not doing any harm, but in my half-sleep I thought I should be doing something about it.

When morning came I still was not rested. Instead of a deep sleep, I had had that troubled half-listening kind. We climbed out of bed and hurried into our clothes. Then I went over and peeked behind the curtain. No one was there. But even as I stood looking at the landlord's boxes and empty bed, I heard a man yawn and stretch. He was our neighbor! His house was so close, the walls so thin, that as far as noise was concerned, he could have been at the other end of our own room.

Meg's laugh came first. We sure had been fooled that time. As we teased each other about hearing sounds in the middle of the night, I vowed I would not be that lazy again. Next time I would look and see if the danger was real or imagined.

But it was good we were up early, it gave us time to get the house straightened before having visitors. Our new landlord and his family came over to greet us. Besides the man and his wife there were five daughters and a son. They were comfortable people to have around. They chatted to us or each other about anything that came into their heads. Typical was the time they gently teased the littlest one about being a witch.

"Why are you calling her a witch?" I asked.

"Her dress is wrong side out," the rest of the fa-

mily shouted. The little girl snuggled closer to her
big sister, knowing that the spotlight would soon
move on to someone else.

It did. But before we were really acquainted with
them, Meg and I had to leave for Chalco to encourage the believers there. When the Cowans were
there, we had stayed in Río Sancho, but George had
been made director and his duties kept him in
Mexico City.

While the Cowans were gone, we stayed in their
house, using both the old one that we had rented
from Catarina, and the new "bedroom" house that
George had built. During the day we were in the
old house teaching and doing medical work. It
was only at night that we spent any time in the
other house.

We usually went over together, but one night
Meg preceded me by a couple of minutes. When
I came up, she was standing in the doorway with a
peculiar smile on her face.

"What's the matter?" I asked.

Very softly she answered, "Someone has been in
here."

At first I wondered what had made her think so.
Then I became aware of a smell of cigarettes. No
one ever smoked in that house. We stood quietly,
methodically looking over the whole room. The
curtain that usually covered the opening to the
clothing boxes was jammed to one side. Well, I
could have left it that way. In the further corner
was a bar from which we hung our clothes. The
Cowans had left some of their clothes there and to
keep them free from dust they had wrapped them

in a sheet. That sheet had been pulled aside. Neither Meg nor I would have touched the Cowans' clothes. Someone searching for something had done that. Fifty pesos had been stolen from us a few months before; maybe the same man was back.

We continued to stand, trying to check everything before we ourselves inadvertently moved it.

"Look!" said Meg. There beyond the bed was a cigarette butt. Someone had indeed been there.

We could not see any other signs from the doorway, so we went in and looked behind curtains and in every corner. Nothing seemed to be missing. We looked again more carefully.

"Let us go to bed," I said; "whoever was here has gone by now."

"How do you know he has gone?" Meg asked.

I was amazed at her question. "But, Meg, we have looked every place."

"We have not looked upstairs."

"There is nothing upstairs a man would want." In order to make more storage space, George had put boards across the rafters, making a platform over our heads. A narrow stairway went up to it.

I remembered the wakeful night I had spent in Río Sancho, and I determined not to have another. Because I wanted a good night's sleep, I climbed the stairs. And stopped. Stretched out in the aisle between the rows of storage boxes was a man sound asleep.

I did not really believe it. I wondered if my imagination was playing tricks on me. No. When I turned around and told Meg, my protesting voice had changed to a gentle one.

It was ten o'clock at night. All the neighbors were in bed, but this was one situation we were not prepared to handle by ourselves. We hurried down to our landlord's house. "Catarina," I called again. I tried several times before getting a sleepy response. "There is a man in our house," I told her.

With an exclamation Catarina and Esteban sprang up. Esteban picked up his machete, Catarina a hoe, and as they came out Catarina leaned over and shook Tomás. He followed with a club.

When Esteban went up the stairs, I was right at his heels. He crept up on the man, his machete raised for action. It made me nervous. I did not want to see a man cut up even if he had broken into my house. Closer and closer Esteban went. Then he relaxed and with contempt his toe poked the sleeping man's ribs. He had recognized him as one of our near neighbors. It took considerable poking before the man stirred. He had been drunk when he broke in, and he had fallen asleep before finding anything valuable. Now he was so ashamed that he could hardly make his way down the steep stairs. He came slowly and every step of the way he had to listen to Catarina's sharp tongue.

"Is it right that we enter other people's houses? Even when we are drunk, is it right?"

Esteban broke in with, "What kind of a man are you? Do you not know that not even a thief steals from his neighbor? If you want to steal, go do it in some other part of town." We could hear the scolding continue even after we had shut the door, and locked it for the night.

Catarina and Esteban had their faults, but they

certainly did their best to take care of us. Meg and
I thanked the Lord for them that night. I thanked
the Lord too, that He had prepared me in advance
for the intruder that He had known was coming.

CHAPTER XXII

Granny and Rafael

(SPRING OF 1948)

BACK AGAIN IN RIO SANCHO, Meg and I spent more and more time visiting in the homes of the people. We had always been especially welcomed by Granny, Lino's mother. Perhaps she had more time than other people because her age excused her from the backbreaking work of harvesting coffee. Perhaps she was such an expert hostess that she succeeded in giving the impression that her work was not pressing. Anyway, whenever we visited her, she stopped whatever she was doing and got chairs for us and a mat for herself. Then she sat at our knees, listening while we sang or talked to her.

One day I reminded her that since she was a child of God, she had the right to call Him "Father," and I suggested that she pray. She did. She told the Lord, "I choose Your road. I do not want any other. You have forgiven me, and I am called Your child." But she did one thing that disturbed me. At every pause in her prayer, she said fervently, "Jesus! Mary!"

After about the third time, I could hardly stand it. I opened my eyes and looked at her. Sweet little old lady—eyes shut tight, hands clasped, praying fervently. I bowed my head again. She had been associating those two names for a long time. I figured that the Holy Spirit would teach her that she was not to call on Mary. I did not want to hurt her feelings.

About a week later I heard her pray again, and she still interspersed her prayer with, "Jesus. Mary." Then I remembered that perhaps the Holy Spirit was depending on me to tell her.

The next time I went back, I was prepared to help her with Scripture. I quoted from Acts 4:12: "Neither is there salvation in any other: for there is none other name under heaven given among men, whereby we must be saved." Then I added, "Mary's name will not save you." And I followed it with John 16:23: "Whatsoever ye ask the Father in my name, he will give it you." I explained, "It is Christ who paid your sin bill; it is His name that counts."

Very quietly she answered, "Thank you for telling me. I cannot read, how was I to know? I am just an illiterate person. I would not know any of this if you had not told me."

The lesson was over and she went to the corner of the room where three big stones clustered around a heap of wood ashes. Sticks of wood, each with one end in the ashes, were lying like spokes in a wheel around the stones. A few years earlier, I would have guessed the fire to be completely out. By now I knew that Granny could bring that fire back almost as easily as someone back home could find a match and light a gas burner. She pushed the sticks until the ends were close together at the center. Then she blew directly on those ends. They glowed, the glow grew brighter, and then flames sprang out from it. With one hand Granny held her small clay pot, with the other she adjusted the stones until the space between them was just right, then carefully she set the pot down upon them. The flames danced against it, and I knew that soon I would have a cup of coffee.

I enjoyed Granny's coffee—she put more sugar in it than most folks did. But more than that I enjoyed watching the skill with which she performed her household tasks. As soon as the coffee was hot, she slowed the fire down by pulling the sticks back until the ends in the center were separated. She left it that way while I drank my first cup. Then as soon as I had finished, she urged me to have a second, but when she saw that I was completely satisfied, she picked up one stick after another and beat the end on the dirt floor. When the red embers faded to gray, she stopped, and put the stick back for use at another time. Care of the fire was such a part of her daily life that her actions were almost mechanical, but I was impressed by the clever way she had saved the firewood.

Firewood was not easy to get even in Río Sancho. Most of the men walked at least an hour before they started cutting any wood, and then they would carry it home on their backs—or if they were more fortunate, they would load it on a donkey. Getting firewood was almost a daily job for some of them, and by the time the boys had become men they tied a load on a donkey easily and well.

Loads were divided in two, half on one side of the donkey, and half on the other, and as long as the two halves weighed the same, there was very little trouble. But whenever one side was heavier than the other, the heavy side tended to slide down while the lighter side came up. That was hard on the donkey, it not only put him off balance, but sometimes chafed him. I had seen Ricardo, one of Lino's servants, take care of such a situation by tying a rock on the lighter side—an interesting way to ease a load on a donkey.

Ricardo was one of the young fellows who frequently dropped in to sing hymns and listen to a Bible lesson. He had heard many times that the Lord loved him, that He was interested in him, and wanted him to live a clean life, but in spite of having heard he still lied when convenient, and had been caught stealing coffee from Lino. It seemed to me that if he had really believed in the Lord that he would have stopped doing such things. I thought back over the lessons and wondered if there was something important that I had left out.

I knew I had told him that the sun was not God, but the Mazatecs believed it so thoroughly, that some of them did not seem to hear any statement to the contrary. So a few days later I tried again; speaking gently I said, "The sun is not God; Jesus Christ is the One we should worship."

This time Ricardo at least heard the words, but he answered belligerently, "The sun is more important than Jesus Christ! I worship the sun!"

I answered, "Jesus is much more important. He died for us; He gives us life; He is God."

Ricardo snorted. "If there were no sun, the corn would not grow; we would die."

In a flash of helplessness I remembered that when I mentioned "Jesus Christ," Ricardo may have thought that I was talking about a picture called by that name. A tremendous sense of shame crept over me—had my witness degenerated into an argument? And did Ricardo think that I was on the side of a lifeless picture?

I tried again. "The real God is Jesus Christ. He is alive and powerful. He *made* the sun."

But again I failed. This time Ricardo rebuked me for saying *sun* without a title of respect. "We call him Father Sun," he told me.

Perhaps the reason Ricardo had not objected before was because the people often equated "Jesus Christ" with the sun. It was when I insisted on a distinction between the two that he objected. I knew of no way I could convince him, and I was glad that we could depend on the Holy Spirit to help.

Once in a while we had the joy of seeing the results of the Holy Spirit's help. We could see progress most easily when we looked at Rafael and Celia. They had begun gathering their children around them every evening while he read a bit from the Bible, then she prayed in Spanish, and he in Mazatec.

I went calling on them twice a week, and in order to encourage them to further Bible study I would say, "Show me something pretty." They could usually do it. One time they turned to the portion on the resurrection, and another time to Ephesians 5. He liked verse 28 especially well. "So ought men to love their wives as their own bodies.

He that loveth his wife loveth himself." His comment was, "The men who beat their wives ought to hear that."

He stood up and stretched out one arm. With the other hand he pointed to it and asked, "Would a man beat his own arm?" Celia and I shook our heads. "Then why should he beat his wife?" Celia became busy with her apron—I suspect she had been beaten in the past. Rafael sat down again and with a chuckle of approval said, "This Book tells about everything."

Rafael was working long hard days with the coffee harvest, but he read the Scriptures just the same. Celia said of him, "He gets tired working, then he prays and that rests him."

Usually only Celia was at home when I went calling, but if I did happen to go when Rafael was there, he could not keep silent. He was bursting to tell about his conversation with this man, and with that one. At such times I would just sit and listen. Talking with one man he had said, "How do I know that this Book is true? I will tell you how. It says that when we believe in Jesus Christ that He will clean us up. I know He has because I do not have the same thoughts that I did before. I am not the same as I used to be."

Rafael had a big oven in the back of his yard, and once a week he would make bread for sale. When someone came to buy, Celia would slip up behind Rafael and say, "Tell him what you just read." Or she would be more specific, "Tell him about the man who took a piece of wood and cooked his bread with one-half and worshiped the other." So Rafael told his customer about Isaiah 44:15-17, and he made his lesson more graphic with, "Pinch it and see if it will holler. Why worship something that cannot even holler when you pinch it?"

I do not know how many people he talked to, but one day after I had walked through the village market with his oldest daughter she said to me, "Did you notice that man standing near the boy who was selling bananas?" I had not noticed but she went on anyway. "He is very much interested in the Word of God." He had been calling at the house to read with Rafael. I wished she had told me when we were there, I would have been thrilled to see anyone who had been taught things in the Bible by another Mazatec.

CHAPTER XXIII

Shoes and Tea

(SPRING OF 1948)

WHEN WE HAD DECIDED to stay on in Río Sancho, Meg and I had agreed that we would spend Monday through Friday there, and the weekend in Chalco. The trip over took us about three and a half hours—less on cloudy days because we walked fast, more on sunny days because we tired in the heat, and much more on rainy days because we slipped in the mud. We never knew whether the day would be hot or cold, since we were in typical high-altitude weather. It was cold when cloudy, hot in the sun.

Our favorite time to travel was early morning. I liked walking in the cool part of the day; Meg liked it because the birds were busy about their business and we could watch them while walking. Actually we stopped walking and watched, then started up again. Probably we did not lose much time that way because the road was uphill and we had to make a certain number of puffing-stops anyway. It was just that Meg arranged to puff where a bird was handy.

I had not known much about birds before, but I guess nobody could have withstood Meg's enthusiasm. As we climbed up from the river through the coffee trees, she would say, "See how nervous that bird is? It is a warbler." When we were out of the coffee trees, she would point to a dead mulberry tree in the middle of a cornfield and say, "See that bird way out on the end of the branch? You can tell he is a flycatcher by the way he sits and then darts."

After the cornfields, we came to a rocky part. No trees, hardly any corn, just rocks. We were too busy choosing our footing to watch for birds there, but one bird let us know he was around even if we were walking with head down and hands hanging at our knees. His song started high and sharp but softened as it came down the scale. Meg never tired of identifying songs for me, but she did not know that bird's voice. It was a long time before we learned that it was a canyon wren who had been keeping us company.

By the time we were beyond the rocks, the sun was high and the birds had disappeared—mysteriously it seemed to me—but Meg insisted that they were just resting under a leaf, or in the grass some place.

With our attention no longer on the birds, we had more time to notice our own feet. Mine usually did pretty well—no blisters, no sprained ankles. But my shoes were having trouble. The sharp rocks cut them, and the mud and water were only slightly less hard on them. Four trips between the two towns was about all a pair could take. After a hole had developed between the sole and the top, the water swished in and out with each step—but they were still usable. However a sole detached all the way around made walking difficult. Twice on that birdless stretch I had walked, stepping high with one foot, trying to put it down with the sole under my toes and not back at the heel.

Meg's shoes were doing better. She had a pair of boots and they had been tough enough to withstand the rocks. I did not own a pair because I had never liked them; they seemed too heavy for comfortable walking. However, when one pair after another of my ordinary shoes had fallen apart on the trail, I got out a pair of rubbers. They were the same pair I had stopped wearing ten years before, and they must have been tired, for they lasted only one trip.

Of course we could have stayed in just one town instead of going back and forth between two, but it seemed to us that new believers in both towns needed teaching.

In Chalco Margarita had been showing interest. She was the woman who had come for help when the blind woman was gored by the bull. At that time she read very poorly, but she wanted to read the Gospel and she struggled to learn. She used to come to our house every Sunday to sing hymns and study with us from the Book of Mark. When we congratulated her for the progress she had made, she answered, "I sit up with it." In other words, she had been reading at night after her day's work was done.

Another who came was Prisca, the one who had gone to Mexico City with us. And Ida who had tried to teach us to whistle. Tomás was ashamed to sing; his voice was in that in-between stage—neither a boy's nor a man's—but he came and brought a pal

with him. Marcos was no longer there. He had
finally rebelled against Esteban's heavy hand. He
had left home and Catarina did not even know
where he was. Tomás had taken over Marcos' work
and he had lost much of his exuberance. He was
tired and unhappy. We watched him, wondering
how we could help.

We did not want to miss our Sunday times with
the Chalco folks, but neither did we want to leave
those in Río Sancho. It seemed to me there was
just one answer and I told it to Meg. "I will pray
that this last pair of shoes does not wear out."

Meg was startled. "Would it not be better to ask
the Lord for more money with which to buy new
ones?"

"There is no place to buy any out here. More
money would not help that. I just need to have
these shoes not wear out." It seemed like a sensible
thing to ask since the Lord had ordered us, "Feed
my sheep," and I needed shoes if I were to do it.

But a trusted friend of Meg's had told her that
we should not expect the Lord to break the laws
of nature. That is, that we should ask for only those
things which He could give us without going
against those laws.

I got out my Bible and read Deuteronomy 29:5:
"And I have led you forty years in the wilderness:
your clothes are not waxen old upon you, and thy
shoe is not waxen old upon thy foot." My answer
was, "If He did that for the Israelites, why can He
no do it for me?"

Meg's friend had talked about dispensations. It
meant that I was not in the same dispensation that

the Israelites had been living in. For some reason or other, according to Meg's friend, the Lord had stopped breaking the laws of nature when the dispensation changed.

The conversation troubled me. How could I pray if I had to know beforehand just what means He would use to answer? My knowledge of science was so slight! I did not know what would be permissible and what was not. "Nonsense!" I said to myself and got ready to pray. But the ask-and-expect-to-get attitude was gone. The quotations about dispensations and science kept ringing in my ears.

Fortunately we would not be taking the trail for another week anyway. We had already planned to stay over in Chalco to meet George Cowan and four staff members of the Young Life organization. These men had come down from the States in order to get a glimpse of the mission field. They hoped that their teaching of the high school crowd would be more forceful if they themselves knew what a mission field looked like. George was taking time off from his duties as director to bring them out from Mexico City.

Meg and I looked at the food on our shelves and tried to figure out what we would feed them. We had sent to the city for an order of groceries, and were expecting it any day, but until it arrived we had very few canned goods. The thing that concerned us most was that we were low in tea. There was no place in town to buy any, and all we could do was hope that the grocery order would arrive before the men did. But it did not.

The men came in that Saturday afternoon. They

had been in the rain most of the ten hours they had been on the trail, and they were cold. They could not get warmed up very fast in our house with mist blowing in through the window. The best we could do was build a charcoal fire in a brazier made from a five-gallon kerosene tin. The men crowded around, slowly turning first one side and then the other to the fire.

Meg and I saw them politely trying to hide their shivers and decided that they were worthy of the last of the tea, so without a word Meg dumped all we had into the pot. Knowing we could not get more, I watched more closely than usual and noticed that the four visitors as well as George were all tea drinkers. Each one had four or five cups apiece.

The tea did help, and as soon as they had warmed up, George took them out to see the town, to meet some of the believers, and some of our friends who were not. In fact, George kept the men so busy that we hardly saw them except at mealtimes.

We had been disappointed at breakfast to see that they did not enjoy coffee. Perhaps that was because we had served them coffee made from beans roasted the Mazatec way. That is, roasted until almost black, and then ground to a powder. Whatever the reason, we could see that they would prefer tea for dinner.

Something had kept me from throwing out the leaves the night before, and we did not have any others, so we made tea with the same ones by putting them on to boil a minute or two. The men did not notice any difference, and I did not either—it was good! The men averaged three cups apiece that day.

On Monday George took them over to see the town of Río Sancho but before they left they had dinner and tea made for the third time from the same leaves. As we served the table I was beginning to wonder, could it be possible that the Lord was answering our questions about Him relative to the laws of nature? Everybody knows that tea leaves are not supposed to act like that! If the Lord could make a good-tasting tea from twice-used leaves, He could keep shoes from wearing out.

Meg was having similar thoughts, and we both looked forward to the men's return on Tuesday and the chance to serve them tea again. We had not told them about our widow's cruse; it was almost too precious to discuss even between the two of us. We just watched, delighted with their, "Another cup, please."

The men were planning to leave at 4:00 A.M. on Wednesday and we intended to have coffee for breakfast, so as I cleared the table Tuesday evening, I looked at the leaves almost lovingly and thought, "Their duty is done"—but I did not throw them out.

We set the alarm and the next morning had the coffee hot, cereal cooked, and eggs ready for the pan when the men arrived from their sleeping quarters. We were urging them to the table when one of them said, "I have an upset stomach this morning. May I have a cup of tea instead of coffee?"

"Surely," I answered, and breathed a prayer of

thanks for the same old leaves. Again I boiled
them. The man drank and was satisfied.

They did not get off at four o'clock; the promised
mules arrived late, but they were gone before we
went for our mail at noon. When we saw what was
in it we chuckled with delight at the Lord's timing.
He must have been trying to teach us a lesson, because there was our grocery order. We tore it open
and, sure enough, there was half a pound of tea.

Our drink was made with new leaves that evening, but it did not taste any better than the tea
we had been having the last four days. Then we
began to wonder, had we been wasting money all
those years? Why buy so much tea? Why not use
the same leaves at least twice? So we saved those
Wednesday night leaves and used them on Thurs-
day. But that tea was terrible! Maybe we should
have boiled them. So we had new leaves on Friday
—and that was good tea. Then we boiled them for
Saturday's tea—and it was not good at all. There
was no question about it. The previous Saturday's
leaves that we had reused on Sunday, Monday,
Tuesday, and Wednesday, had been special—made
that way by the Lord.

What a loving, gentle heavenly Father we have!
My faith had wavered, and while I had been
troubled, He had answered in a way I would never
have thought of asking. I was no longer troubled
by "dispensations" and "laws of nature." I knew
that the Lord was ready to help me no matter what
it involved.

Meg had learned too, in fact, she was more courageous about it than I was. She wrote a tract telling people about the tea incident. I shyly kept it to myself awhile.

Oh, yes, my shoes withstood the trail. They lasted until I was in the city and able to buy more.

CHAPTER XXIV

The Word at Work

(SPRING OF 1949)

FLORRIE AND GEORGE COWAN had proofread the
Book of Acts and I John while Meg and I were
away from the tribe. The American Bible Society
had published them and they were ready for us to
take back in the spring of 1949. With delight we
packed some in our hand baggage in order to have
them ready for use on our trip in.

Tepetlán, the town in which we changed from
truck to mule, was the first place in which there
were any Mazatecs. For the most part, the people
there were Spanish-speaking. A few Mazatecs came
to town to sell their coffee harvest, to buy a supply
of corn, or to buy other things not available in
Chalco. Those Mazatecs were the ones we might
meet on the street, but there were others whom we
were less apt to meet. They were the ones in the
county jail.

Each little Mazatec town had its own jail, but
that was for minor offenses—wife-beating, drunkenness, disobedience to some town rule. For the most
part, the men in the county jail were there for murder, or for having been connected in some way with
murder. That did not mean they would be in jail

for the rest of their lives, but at least they would be in there a year.

Meg and I began to think about those men. Maybe they would be just the ones to read Acts and I John. Previously we had tried to get men to read the Gospel of Mark. Most of them claimed to be interested, but many of them said, "I would like to read it, but I am too busy." At least the men in the jail could not say that. The more we thought about it, the more it seemed right that the jail should have copies of the new books.

That was undoubtedly a good idea, but I did not want to take them there. I knew how conspicuous two American girls would be walking into a place like that.

But how could we pass through a town with Scripture in our hands and not leave it with the Mazatec men who had time to read it? To do such a thing just did not seem right. Meg and I got out the books and decided that we would at least walk by and see what the jail looked like.

It was a big high-walled building just off the town square. The day was Tuesday, market day, and the square was crowded with people buying and selling their merchandise. The people watched us and nudged each other as we walked down the sidewalk. When I saw it I thought, "We cannot go today, it would cause too much commotion. It would be better on some day other than market day."

We turned the corner at the far side of the square and then we could see the entrance. The big barn-like door was open and about twenty feet inside was

an iron gate shutting off a courtyard. Prisoners
were allowed to come up to the gate and look out.
As we walked slowly past, someone was there who
recognized us. His reaction was a hushed exclamation. Then he motioned for us to come. We went
by but I heard the short sharp whistle with which
he called others to the gate.

We were embarrassed in front of people in the
market, but we had been praying for those men,
so we turned and went past for another look. This
time the gate was jammed with faces—about twenty
of them, and arms through the bars were beckoning.
Softly, urgently they called, not in the Spanish language of the people in the square, but in our own
mountain Mazatec. They were our folks! We
stepped around the man selling tomatoes, smiled
at the woman offering us oranges, walked through
the big wooden doors and in Mazatec fashion we
touched finger tips with the men behind the gate.

Once the customary "hello" had been said we
were besieged with questions, everybody talking at
once. They wanted to know where we had been,
where we were going, how long we would be in
Tepetlán, and how long we would stay in Chalco.
Even though several had asked the same question,
they were not satisfied with a general answer to the
crowd. Each one wanted the answer to his question
to be directed specifically to him.

Their insistent voices controlled the conversation,
and I thought, "This is no place to try to teach anyone about the Lord," and I wanted to leave. But
I had gone in to give the men copies of the newly
printed portions of the Bible and I could at least

do that. I opened I John at chapter 2 and started to read in the middle of verse 1: "And if any man sin, we have an advocate with the Father, Jesus Christ the righteous."

Instantly the place became so silent that the sound of my own voice startled me. The men were listening. We went on to verses 2 and 3. I wanted them to read it for themselves, so we passed copies in to those who knew how. Then it was Meg and I who were hanging on the gate, and our arms went through the bars as we pointed to the words in the books the men were holding.

Several of them could read simple words in Spanish, but it would take persistence on their part if they were to learn to read the Gospel in Mazatec. Attentively, respectfully they listened and tried. I forgot the market behind us as we went on reading and explaining portions in the Epistle of John and in Acts. A little girl came to sell *tortillas* to the men. They were in the habit of buying food from her, but this time they did not want to be disturbed; they were busy listening and they did not want to be interrupted.

As we finished reading, I looked at the men more carefully. I did not recognize any as from Chalco or Río Sancho, but they all looked Mazatec. I knew that the district served by the jail included at least one Mixtec town, some Aztec towns, and a few Spanish-speaking places. I was puzzled; why had only Mazatec-speaking prisoners come out to greet us? So I asked, "Do all of you here speak Mazatec?" I should not have asked. They were embarrassed for their tribe. Nobody answered, they just looked down at the ground. I tried to hurry on, "I do not know you; are you all from Chalco?"

Heads came up and they indicated one of those who had read best. "He is from Tetitla." I looked and silently prayed a little extra for him—maybe he could tell the people of Tetitla about the Lord.

"That one is from Ninitlán." We all looked in his direction. He had not said very much, maybe because his dialect was different from the rest of us.

"That fellow over there is from San Luis." No wonder he had stayed at the outer edge of the group; his town was despised by the other Mazatecs.

Then I realized that at the jail were representatives from many parts of the tribe. By going there we had contacted a number of them at the same time. It was good that we had made our feet bring us in, certainly there could not have been a better place to start using the new portions of Scripture.

As we turned to leave, we saw that the guards were watching us from a room off at the right, and our "good-bye" included them as well as the prisoners. We stepped out into the square and found that the people there were smiling friendly sympathetic smiles. They knew we were from Chalco and it had seemed fitting to them that we call on our fellow townspeople—and maybe it was. However, we preferred to be with them when they were in their home environment, and we were glad to arrive there the next day.

One of our first visitors was a woman who was concerned about her dead son. He had committed murder, so she figured that his punishment in the afterlife was probably pretty hard. I did not enjoy answering her questions. I tried, but I could not think of anything hopeful to say about a nonbelieving man who was already dead. The best I could do was to tell her that she should be concerned for her family before they died. They should know while they were still alive that Jesus was the road to Heaven. Her answer was, "I will go down right now and tell my son Milio."

I offered to show her the type of thing he needed to know, and when she told me that he could read, I got out a copy of I John. We went over I John 5:11, 12 together: "And this is the record, that God hath given to us eternal life, and this life is in his Son. He that hath the Son hath life; and he that hath not the Son of God hath not life."

The book had so many verses that were valuable to a man about to believe, that I was afraid I would confuse her if we studied them all. So I just pointed out a few that she should show him, and I hoped that he would be interested enough to read the rest by himself.

About two weeks later a nice-looking young man came up and spoke to me through the window. "There are two people here who would like to meet you," he said.

"Let them come in," I answered. Then I realized that in asking for an invitation for his friends, he had received one for himself as well.

In a minute he was back with two other young fellows. Their spokesman looked familiar but I could not place him. He saw that I was puzzled so he explained, "I was in jail and you visited me."

With that much help I recognized him. He was the one from Tetitla who had read so well.

Very gently, as though he did not want to hurt my feelings, he told me, "Your religion is despised by our people. They do not say the things that you say. But now we have come to ask you to tell us about the things that you believe." And he started by asking about verses he had read in Acts and I John.

We talked, led on by his questions, for an hour and a half. His friends did not say much, but they listened carefully, and I was thrilled with the indication that seed sown in the jail was bringing forth fruit from among a people living in a town a fifteen-hour walk from it.

The struggle for words had taken the Cowans and the rest of us years. But it had been worth it. Now with three books of the Bible in print, we could use those Scriptures as we witnessed, and the people could read them for themselves and to each other. We knew it was good seed, and in Isaiah 30:23 the Lord had said that He would give rain for the seed with which we sow the ground. He had done so.